GUIDELINES FOR RESPONDING TO STUDENT THREATS OF VIOLENCE

Dewey G. Cornell, Ph.D.
Peter L. Sheras, Ph.D.

A manual for school-based teams to assess and respond effectively to students who threaten violence

SOPRIS WEST EDUCATIONAL SERVICES
A CAMBIUM LEARNING COMPANY

BOSTON, MA • NEW YORK, NY • LONGMONT, CO

ISBN 13: 978-1-59318-502-2
ISBN 10: 1-59318-502-2
JDE #: 112301/9-13

Printed in the United States of America
Published and Distributed by

Sopris West®
EDUCATIONAL SERVICES

A Cambium Learning® Company

4093 Specialty Place • Longmont, Colorado 80504
(303) 651-2829 • www.sopriswest.com

"Drs. Cornell and Sheras present a blend of research and practical application. Their recognition and involvement of School Resource Officers is especially refreshing since SROs are too often under-acknowledged for the important role they play in working with school staff to assess and manage student threats. The case studies and practical exercises take threat assessment principles beyond the generic rhetoric of many post-Columbine ⬚expert' publications to a new level of resource for practical application."

Kenneth S. Trump, M.P.A., President
National School Safety and Security Services

"Our school division has used the threat assessment guidelines for the past four years. The guidelines offer simple steps to evaluate the severity of an incident from horseplay to a very serious expression. I have noticed that my assistant principal and I have been more consistent in our decision making and recommending consequences and support for students and families since implementing the guidelines. We have also noticed greater support and confidence from parents when they realize we are using a research-based model to guide in our decisions."

L. Bernard Hairston, Ph.D., Principal
Burley Middle School, Albemarle County, VA

"Professors Cornell and Sheras challenge many of the commonly accepted myths about dealing with student threats. Best of all, for school practitioners, the book translates our best knowledge into highly readable and eminently usable information for front-line educators faced with the complex task of responding to threats. . . . In sum, this book fills a very significant void in practice. It weaves together scholarly findings and practical suggestions as well as any educational publication I've seen."

Russell Skiba, Ph.D.
Counseling and Educational Psychology
Indiana University

"Cornell and Sheras have done an outstanding job providing school administrators with insightful guidance and suggestions for dealing with student threats. . . . In today's tense climate, this is a ⬚must read' for educators."

Dr. Ronald Stephens, Director
National School Safety Center

"This work has no equal in school-based threat assessment literature. The authors have shown the utmost scholarship and integrity in the development of this resource guide. It is informative, practical, integrates easily into school procedures, and it is backed by objective research. This book is required reading for all school safety teams. It will provide a core resource for the training of my school psychology students. Implementing the procedures described in this guide will not only make schools safer, it will make them more humane and caring."

Michael J. Furlong, Ph.D.
Gevirtz Graduate School of Education
University of California, Santa Barbara

"The format is easy to follow and practical, leading school personnel through all stages of threat assessment implementation. Most importantly, I think that the authors do an outstanding job of communicating the long-successful nature of U.S. Secret Service threat assessment methods...Their approach represents a very important practical contribution to schooling."

Randy Kamphaus, Ph.D.
Department of Educational Psychology
University of Georgia

". . . an excellent practical resource for educational professionals. This book presents straightforward step-by-step activities for school-based practitioners to appropriately assess and effectively respond to students who threaten violence. . . . The forms for threat assessment documentation and behavior support plans included in the book provided a concrete format for gathering information and planning appropriate actions. . . . an essential addition to any professional library."

Shane R. Jimerson, Ph.D.
Counseling, Clinical, and School Psychology
University of California, Santa Barbara

"The Guidelines provides school principals and other staff the rationale and step-by-step process to respond to potentially dangerous students and situations. . . The authors furnish the necessary evidence-based underpinnings required for schools to consider when modifying or creating new programs. . . With wonderful copy-ready sample forms, and clear examples, this book provides all school administrators need to start from scratch or to modify their current program to be truly responsive to the threat of violence in their school building."

Ron Palomares, Ph.D.
Licensed Psychologist, Licensed Specialist in
School Psychology, National Certified School
Psychologist

"Cornell and Sheras have written a definitive and much-needed guide for responding to student threats of violence in schools. While the FBI and Secret Service reports on threat assessment and school shooters were useful sources of information and ideas, this book provides a step by step and practical guide for responding that will be invaluable to school administrators."

"This book is the first complete guide for schools to move from capacity building to threat assessment protocols to data-based decision making and evidence-based student support plans. Cornell and Sheras provide useful and detailed examples throughout the book and an excellent summary of their research on the actual patterns of threats in schools. Every school administrator should use this comprehensive book, and it would be invaluable for use in administrator licensure programs."

Jeffrey Sprague, Ph.D.
Associate Professor of Special Education
Co-Director, University of Oregon Institute on
Violence and Destructive Behavior

Many persons and organizations contributed to our efforts in developing these student threat assessment guidelines. First, we would like to recognize the Jessie Ball duPont Fund for the financial support that made it possible to undertake this project. We also thank the Federal Bureau of Investigation for its 1999 conference on school shootings and the accompanying research and recommendations (O'Toole, 2000) that were foundational to our efforts. We thank the Curry School of Education at the University of Virginia for its support of our organization, the Virginia Youth Violence Project.

We thank the School Work Group from Albemarle County and Charlottesville City Public Schools, which in 2000 helped devise the first draft of the threat assessment guidelines. This group included Carole Hastings, Chris Love, and Frank Morgan from Albemarle County Public Schools; Nancy Cornell, Ron Hutchinson, and Robert Thompson from the City of Charlottesville Public Schools; and Sgt. Jim Bond from the Albemarle County Police Department and Sgt. Allen Kirby from the City of Charlottesville Police Department. We especially appreciate the efforts of Frank Morgan and Ron Hutchinson in facilitating the field testing of the guidelines in their school divisions, and we thank the principals and assistant principals, psychologists, school resource officers, counselors, and other school staff members of the 35 schools that served as our field-test sites.

We benefited from the consultation of our Advisory Board, which included Donna Bowman, Arlene Cundiff, Chip Harding, Kirk Heilbrun, and John Monahan. Mary Ellen O'Toole and Terri Royster of the Federal Bureau of Investigation also provided consultation.

We appreciate the advice and constructive criticism of Julia Blodgett, Randy Borum, Steve Clarke, Michael Furlong, Russ Skiba, and Jeffrey Sprague. We thank Barbara Nordin for her editing assistance.

We express our appreciation to the doctoral students in the Programs in Clinical and School Psychology at the University of Virginia's Curry School of Education. The graduate students who assisted in our research at the outset were Andrea Levy-Elkon, Sebastian Kaplan, David McConville, Lela McKnight, and Julea Posey Douglass; they were joined in later years by Julie Amato, Chris Branson, Joanna Cole, Bernice Joo, Peter Thunfors, and Farah Williams and most recently by Lauren Ashbaugh and Megan Eliot.

Diana Browning Wright has played an invaluable role in encouraging and critiquing our guidelines, as well as in initiating their use in California public schools. Her work in training school staff around the country to conduct functional analyses of behavior and develop behavior support plans led us to invite her to coauthor Chapter 10 on student interventions.

Dewey G. Cornell, Ph.D., is a clinical psychologist and Professor of Education in the Curry School of Education at the University of Virginia (U.Va.). Dr. Cornell is Director of the U.Va. Youth Violence Project and is a faculty associate of the Institute of Law, Psychiatry, and Public Policy. Dr. Cornell has studied youth violence and conducted forensic evaluations of juvenile offenders since 1984. He is the author or coauthor of more than 100 professional publications in psychology and education, including research on juvenile homicide, psychological assessment, and school safety.

Peter L. Sheras, Ph.D., is the Associate Director for Instruction of the Virginia Youth Violence Project and Professor in the Curry Programs in Clinical and School Psychology at the University of Virginia's Curry School of Education. His work with adolescents, couples, and families includes service as a co-coordinator of the Charlottesville/Albemarle School Crisis Network and as a member of the Phi Delta Kappa National Task Force on Adolescent Suicide. He served on the national expert panel that produced "Early Warning: A Timely Response" for the U.S. Department of Education. Dr. Sheras is a licensed clinical psychologist and counsels and lectures in the area of parenting adolescent children. He is the author of books and articles on bullying, adolescent behavior, youth violence, and parenting. He is the coauthor of the "Stress Index for Parents of Adolescents." He works frequently with school systems on crisis response and violence prevention.

CONTENTS

CHAPTER 1 What Is Threat Assessment? 1

CHAPTER 2 The Threat Assessment Team 13

CHAPTER 3 Beginning the Threat Assessment 19

CHAPTER 4 Responding to Substantive Threats 29

CHAPTER 5 Mental Health Assessment of Threatening Students 39

CHAPTER 6 Pathways to Youth Violence 53

CHAPTER 7 Frequently Asked Questions 59

CHAPTER 8 Research Findings 71

CHAPTER 9 Schoolwide Violence Prevention 83

CHAPTER 10 Interventions After a Student Threat of Violence 91
By Diana Browning Wright and Dewey Cornell

CHAPTER 11 Implementing Threat Assessment 101

APPENDIX Threat Assessment Documentation 110

Behavior Support Plan 114

Behavior Support Plan—Case Examples 119

Test Your Knowledge of These Guidelines 131

References 139

CHAPTER 1

WHAT IS THREAT ASSESSMENT?

PURPOSE

The purpose of this manual is to provide practical guidelines for school-based teams to conduct threat assessments of students who threaten to commit an act of violence. As team leader, a school administrator—principal or assistant principal—can use these guidelines to conduct a preliminary assessment of the seriousness of a student's threat and determine whether the threat can be quickly resolved or will require more extensive evaluation and intervention. In more serious cases, the full threat assessment team—typically consisting of the principal or assistant principal, school resource officer, psychologist, and counselor—can use the guidelines in determining what steps to take in order to prevent an act of violence. From a legal liability perspective, these guidelines provide school divisions with a means of demonstrating that they have adhered to the developing standard of care in responding to potentially dangerous students.

GOALS

The goals of threat assessment are twofold: (1) to maintain a safe school environment by preventing an act of violence from taking place, and (2) to resolve student conflicts or problems that underlie threatening behavior. Violence prevention is always the first goal of threat assessment, but it is also important to determine why a student made a threat and to address whatever conflict or problem motivated the threat. Ultimately, successful resolution of the student's conflict or problem will contribute to the first goal of maintaining a safe school environment.

WHAT IS THREAT ASSESSMENT?

Threat assessment is an approach to violence prevention originally developed by the U.S. Secret Service based on studies of persons who attacked or threatened to attack public officials (Fein, Vossekuil, & Holden, 1995; Fein & Vossekuil, 1999). Threat assessment was soon recognized as a way to analyze a wide range of potentially violent situations (Fein & Vossekuil, 1998; O'Toole, 2000; Reddy et al., 2001). In 1999, the FBI's National Center for the Analysis of Violent Crime convened a national conference on school shootings and subsequently issued a report (O'Toole, 2000) concluding that schools should use a threat assessment approach. In 2002, a joint report of the U.S. Secret Service and Department of Education recommended that schools train

---

WHAT IS A THREAT?

A threat is *an expression of intent to harm someone.* Threats may be spoken, written, or expressed in some other way, such as through gestures. Threats may be direct ("I am going to beat you up") or indirect ("I'm going to get him"). Illegal possession of weapons should be presumed to indicate a threat unless careful investigation reveals otherwise (e.g., a student accidentally brought a knife to school). When in doubt about whether a student's behavior is a threat, evaluate it as a threat.

threat assessment teams in order to respond to student threats of violence (Fein et al., 2002).

A threat assessment is conducted when a person (or persons) threatens to commit a violent act or engages in behavior that appears to threaten an act of violence. This kind of threatened violence is termed "targeted violence." Threat assessment is a process of evaluating the threat and the circumstances surrounding it in order to uncover any evidence that indicates the threat is likely to be carried out.

"Threat assessment" is more than a generic term for investigation of a potentially dangerous situation. Threat assessment in schools is predicated on six principles, which were articulated by the U.S. Secret Service and the Department of Education (Fein et al., 2002). We present our distillation of these principles here (Cornell, 2004).

1. *Prevention is possible.* Targeted violence is not a spontaneous, unpredictable event but is the result of a deliberate and detectable process. Students who commit serious acts of violence do not suddenly "snap" and begin shooting at random; their behavior is preceded by days or weeks of thought and planning, and in many cases they share their ideas and intentions with others (Vossekuil, Fein, Reddy, Borum, & Modzeleski, 2002). This means that targeted school violence can be prevented if enough is known about the student's preparatory behavior.

2. *Consider the context.* Threat assessment must consider not only the student who makes the threat, but also the total context of the threat. This includes the situation in which the threat was made and what the student intended by making the threat. Many times a student will make a transient threatening statement as a joke, insult, or rhetorical remark without substantial intent to harm anyone. The context of the student's behavior makes it apparent that the threat is not serious. However, if there is reason to take the threat seriously, a complete threat assessment should consider additional contextual factors. For example, threat assessment should consider the student's prior relationship with

the intended victim and characteristics of the threatened victim (or victims) that might increase or decrease the likelihood that the threat will be carried out.

Threat assessment should include an investigation of the student's current life circumstances and level of distress, because students who commit serious acts of violence may have experienced significant situational stress, such as family problems, separations, or personal losses. Finally, threat assessment must include consideration of the environmental context of the threat. There may be factors in the student's social environment that encourage violence or discourage more appropriate ways of resolving problems or seeking help. For example, several of the school shooters were encouraged by antisocial peers to carry out their attacks. A good threat assessment team attempts to construct a complete picture of the threat in its overall context.

3. *Adopt an investigative mind-set.* School authorities investigating a threat must adopt a critical and skeptical mindset that strives to accumulate reliable evidence and verify all claimed facts about the situation. Their approach must be fair, and they must be willing to accept or reject hypotheses based on a careful analysis of all available information. This principle guards against the potential for school authorities to jump to conclusions that a student is dangerous based on rumor or unverified allegations.

> There is no set of psychological characteristics that unequivocally indicates future violence in the absence of specific observations that the student is preparing to commit an act of violence.

4. *Rely on facts, not profiles.* Conclusions must be based on objective facts and behaviors rather than inferred traits or characteristics of the student making the threat. This

principle explicitly contradicts the effort to make judgments based on a hypothetical profile of the violent student.

5. *Gather information from multiple sources.* In serious cases, information should be gathered from multiple sources within and outside the school system. There may be teachers, counselors, or other school personnel or students who have information that should be considered. An "integrated systems approach" to investigation seeks cooperation with law enforcement, social service agencies, mental health providers, religious organizations, and other groups or organizations in the community. This principle requires the school to look beyond its own boundaries and to use all available resources rather than to function as a closed and isolated system.

6. *Does the student pose a threat?* Threat assessment is ultimately concerned with whether the student *poses* a threat, not whether the student has *made* a threat. Any student can make a threat, but relatively few will engage in behavior that indicates the planning and preparation necessary to carry out the threat. Threat assessment does not end when a student is found to have made a threat; rather, *threat assessment aims to determine how serious the threat is and then what should be done about it.*

WHY DO WE NEED THREAT ASSESSMENT?

As a result of the fear and concern generated by school shootings, schools need a safe, rational approach to evaluating students who demonstrate potentially dangerous behavior. Media attention to the high-profile school shootings—culminating in the excessive coverage of the Columbine massacre—distorted public perceptions of schools and the risk of homicidal violence to students. Even the most reputable news agencies in the United States bombarded the public with frightening images of bloodied children, anguished parents, and traumatized teachers. Because these images were so vivid and memorable, it was easy to misjudge the prevalence of school violence and overestimate the likelihood of a shooting taking place in one's own school. The public became so sensitized to these incidents that they developed the misperception that our nation's schools were undergoing an epidemic of violence and that school shootings were likely to happen in their own schools (Cornell, 2005; Mulvey & Cauffman, 2001; Trump, 2000).

There was a substantial increase in juvenile violent crime, especially homicide, in the United States from 1983 to 1993 (Federal Bureau of Investigation, 1984–2004). The combination of widespread juvenile access to firearms and the development of the crack cocaine market played a significant role in this increase (U.S. Surgeon General, 2001). Contrary to public perception, juvenile violent crime, including homicide, declined markedly after 1993 (Federal Bureau of Investigation, 1984–2004). Multiple studies of school violence showed similar declines (Cornell, 2005; DeVoe et al., 2004).

In fact, homicides committed by students at school are exceedingly rare in a population of more than 53 million students attending 119,000 public and private schools (U.S. Census Bureau, 2003). According to case reports compiled by the National School Safety Center (2003), 116 persons were murdered by students at school in 93 incidents that took place from the 1992–1993 school year through the 2001–2002 school year (Cornell, 2005). Considering that 93 incidents took place over 10 years, the annual probability of a school experiencing a student-perpetrated homicide is about 1 in 12,804. Nevertheless, school administrators across the country will admit that they have lost sleep worrying that a student at their school might kill someone, and this fear influences their perceptions and their decisions when dealing with an angry or threatening student. Threat assessment offers an alternative to fear-based, subjective reactions to student threats.

Although homicides are rare, other forms of violence are more frequent at school. According to a national survey of school principals (Miller, 2003), in 1999–2000 an estimated 1.5 million

3

violent incidents occurred in public schools; more than 92% of secondary schools, 87% of middle schools, and 61% of elementary schools reported at least one incident. According to the National Crime Victimization Survey, the annual violent crime victimization rate at school was 24 crimes per 1,000 for students 12 to 18 years old (DeVoe et al., 2004). Although student self-reported data must be considered with caution (Cornell, 2005; Cornell & Loper, 1998), results from the Youth Risk Behavior Survey indicate that 13% of students in grades 9–12 reported being in a physical fight, 9% reported being threatened or injured with a weapon, and 6% reported carrying a weapon on school property in the past year (DeVoe et al., 2004). These findings indicate that threat assessment policies should be focused on the kinds of violent incidents that are most likely to occur and should not be skewed by a few high-publicity homicides that are unlikely to occur in the career of any school administrator.

Zero tolerance. The fear of school shootings triggered an extreme reaction in American schools: the expansion of so-called *zero tolerance* policies. Originally, zero tolerance referred to a policy of automatic expulsion of students for bringing a gun to school, promulgated by the Gun-Free Schools Act (1994). As originally conceived, zero tolerance was an appealing concept that won widespread popular support, but over time the policy was expanded to include all weapons and drugs and, in many school divisions, much more. The prohibition of weapons in many school divisions was defined to include toy weapons and objects that appeared to be weapons. For example, a ten-year-old boy was expelled from elementary school because he brought to school a one-inch (2.5-mm) plastic toy pistol that was an accessory to his G.I. Joe® action figure. The boy discovered that he had the tiny toy in his pocket by accident when he checked to see if he had his lunch money (*The Seattle Times,* January 8, 1997). Skiba and Peterson (1999) documented numerous cases of excessive punishment, which they referred to as "the dark side of zero tolerance." Among the examples they cited are these:

- A five-year-old in California was expelled after he found a razor blade at his bus stop, carried it to school, and gave it to his teacher.
- A nine-year-old in Ohio was suspended for having a one-inch knife in a manicure kit.
- A twelve-year-old in Rhode Island was suspended for bringing a toy gun to school.
- A seventeen-year-old in Chicago was arrested and subsequently expelled for shooting a paper clip with a rubber band.

A central problem with zero tolerance policies is that all threats of violence are treated as equally dangerous and deserving of the same consequences, and, in some states, schools are required to have a zero tolerance policy that makes no exceptions (Tebo, 2000). Such policies provide no latitude for school authorities to consider the seriousness of the threat or degree of risk posed by the student's behavior. In 2001, the American Bar Association passed a resolution condemning zero tolerance:

> . . . the ABA opposes, in principle, "zero tolerance" policies that have a discriminatory effect, or mandate either expulsion or referral of students to juvenile or criminal court, without regard to the circumstances or nature of the offense or the student's history.

A 2000 report (*Opportunities Suspended: The Devastating Consequences of Zero Tolerance and School Discipline*) by the Advancement Project and The Civil Rights Project of Harvard University declared, "Zero Tolerance has become a philosophy that has permeated our schools; it employs a brutally strict disciplinary model that embraces harsh punishment over education" (p. 3).

Profiling. Another response to the school shootings was the effort to *profile* seemingly dangerous students before they engage in violence. Profiling is an appealing concept that seems to make sense: draw up a list of the characteristics of dangerous students so that such students can be identified before they commit an act of violence. Accordingly, many governmental agencies and professional organizations devised lists of "warning signs" to identify potentially violent students (American

Psychological Association, 1999; Dwyer, Osher, & Warger, 1998; National School Safety Center, 1998; Sewell & Mendelsohn, 2000).

Unfortunately, the criteria in warning signs checklists tend to cast an overly broad net in identifying potentially violent youth. The 16 warning signs in the federal government's guide *Early Warning, Timely Response* (Dwyer et al., 1998) include such items as "history of discipline problems," "drug use and alcohol use," "feelings of being picked on and persecuted," and "excessive feelings of rejection." The American Psychological Association's (1999) *Warning Signs* pamphlet sounds an ominous note with the statement, "If you see these immediate warning signs, violence is a serious possibility." The list of "immediate warning signs" includes "increase in risk-taking behavior," "increase in use of drugs or alcohol," "significant vandalism or property damage," and "loss of temper on a daily basis." Most school authorities could identify students in their schools who appear to meet these signs yet fail to pose a threat for violence.

Similarly, the National School Safety Center (1998) promulgated a 20-item *Checklist of Characteristics of Youth Who Have Caused School-Associated Violent Deaths*. This checklist includes some very general items, such as "has been previously truant, suspended, or expelled from school," "has little or no supervision from parents or a caring adult," and "tends to blame others for difficulties she or he causes." The items on such checklists may well describe the small group of youths who committed school shootings, but this does not make them useful, specific indicators of violence. Because the base rate for severe violence is low, checklists of student characteristics will invariably lead to the false-positive identification of a very large number of students who will not be violent (Sewell & Mendelsohn, 2000).

The warning signs lists contain items that are deserving of concern; for example, alcohol and drug use is a well-known correlate of delinquency and violence. Items such as losing one's temper on a daily basis or committing acts of vandalism are behaviors that merit intervention. The federal warning signs list (Dwyer et al., 1998) was developed in consultation with a panel of experts,

and the larger document is an excellent resource for schools. The authors of the federal warning signs report recognized the potential problems of a warning signs approach. They cautioned, "Unfortunately, *there is a real danger that early warning signs will be misinterpreted*" (Dwyer et al., 1998, p. 7, italics in the original). These authors urged school authorities to refrain from using the warning signs as a basis for punishing students or excluding them from school. They expressed concern that the warning signs could be used without regard to the student's situational or developmental context. They cautioned against acting on the basis of stereotypes or overreacting to single signs. In follow-up to the warning signs report, Dwyer and Osher (2000) presented an

---

THE FBI ADVOCATES EVALUATING STUDENT THREATS . . .

"Although the risk of an actual shooting incident at any one school is very low, threats of violence are potentially a problem at any school. Once a threat is made, having a fair, rational, and standardized method of evaluating and responding to threats is critically important" (O'Toole, 2000, p. 1).

. . . BUT REJECTS STUDENT PROFILING.

"One response to the pressure for action may be an effort to identify the next shooter by developing a 'profile' of the typical school shooter. This may sound like a reasonable preventive measure, but in practice, trying to draw up a catalogue or 'checklist' of warning signs to detect a potential school shooter can be shortsighted, even dangerous. Such lists, publicized by the media, can end up unfairly labeling many nonviolent students as potentially dangerous or even lethal. In fact, a great many adolescents who will never commit violent acts will show some of the behaviors or personality traits included on the list" (O'Toole, 2000, pp. 2–3).

action guide for schools. The action guide contains thoughtful advice and recommendations for school authorities, and it gives many examples of strategies, interventions, and programs designed to prevent student violence.

In 1999 the FBI's National Center for the Analysis of Violent Crime, a group renowned for its use of criminal profiling, convened a conference on school shootings. The FBI report (O'Toole, 2000) firmly rejected the application of profiling to school shootings, recognizing that school shootings were too rare and that the likelihood of falsely identifying students as dangerous was much too high.

A key finding from the FBI study of school shootings was that, in almost every case, the student shooter communicated his intentions to peers days or weeks in advance of the crime. Had these intentions been reported to authorities, it would have been possible to investigate the threat and prevent the shootings. In support of this conclusion, the FBI found other cases in which school shootings were prevented because students did report a classmate's threats to authorities. These observations led the FBI researchers to conclude that schools should be prepared to identify and evaluate student threats in a prompt and systematic manner.

The FBI report cautioned that "all threats are not created equal" (p. 5) and that each threat must be carefully investigated to determine what danger the student poses to others. Students who make threats differ in their capacities for violence and in their levels of motivation to carry out a violent act. For this reason, the FBI recommended that schools train threat assessment teams.

HOW DOES THREAT ASSESSMENT DIFFER FROM OTHER APPROACHES?

Consider the case of a middle school student named Bob who told some students on the school bus that he was going to kill another student named Casey. One student told the bus driver what Bob said, and the bus driver informed the principal. How should the principal respond? Compare the hypothetical responses of principals in middle schools A, B, and C:

SCHOOL A: ZERO TOLERANCE

In School A, the principal confronted Bob with the alleged threat, and Bob admitted making the statement. The principal needed no further information. According to the school board's zero tolerance policy, a student who threatens to kill someone must be suspended from school for the remainder of the school year. Bob and his parents are left angry and frustrated. His educational record has been ruined. Moreover, nothing has been done to reduce the risk that Bob might carry out his threat. In theory, zero tolerance for threatening behavior seems like a good idea, but, in practice, zero tolerance has been applied in an overly rigid manner because the same sanction is imposed regardless of the circumstances.

SCHOOL B: PROFILING

In School B, the principal confronted Bob with the alleged threat, and again Bob admitted making the statement. Bob angrily said that he was tired of being teased by other students, that nobody liked him, and that he did not want to go to school anyway. The principal consulted an official list of warning signs with items such as "low school interest and poor academic performance," "social withdrawal," "excessive feelings of isolation and being alone," "excessive feelings of rejection," "feelings of being picked on and persecuted," and "uncontrolled anger" (Dwyer et al., 1998). The principal erroneously concluded that Bob fit the general profile of a dangerous student and moved him to an alternative school.

SCHOOL C: THREAT ASSESSMENT

In School C, the principal used a threat assessment approach to consider the context and meaning of the student's behavior. The principal interviewed Bob about the alleged threat, and, when Bob admitted making the threat, the principal asked a series of questions about Bob's intent, including how and why he would carry out the threat. The principal also interviewed several students as sources of corroborating information. At this point in the threat assessment, the principal must decide whether the threat is *transient*, which can be resolved immediately, or *substantive*, which warrants further assessment.

In a typical transient case, the principal might find that Bob used the word "kill" only as a figure of speech because he was mad at Casey over a disagreement they had the previous day. Bob might explain that he had no intention of harming Casey and agree to meet and apologize to Casey. Bob might be suspended from riding the bus for one week as a consequence of making inappropriate statements on the school bus. The principal would meet with all of the students involved in the incident to explain to them that threats to kill someone are not appropriate and will be taken seriously.

If the principal did not conclude that Bob's threat was transient—perhaps because Bob expressed continuing anger toward Casey or was not willing to apologize—then the principal would classify the threat as substantive and, as a result, notify the threat assessment team in order to set into motion a more complex set of actions. If a threat is substantive, the principal must take suitable protective action—starting with contacting the school resource officer, suspending Bob and summoning his parents to come for him, and warning Casey and Casey's parents of Bob's threat. As a member of the threat assessment team, the school resource officer might recommend additional protective actions and also determine whether there was reason to charge Bob with a crime. The school psychologist might evaluate Bob for the purpose of assessing Bob's mental state and finding out what happened between him and Casey. The school counselor or other team members might identify suitable interventions for Bob, such as a conflict mediation program or individual counseling to address Bob's anger and aggression. Under most circumstances, the threat assessment team would develop a plan that would permit Bob to eventually return to school or to continue his education in an alternative setting.

In this hypothetical situation, threat assessment offers a more flexible and less punitive response to Bob's threat than a zero tolerance approach. In what we term "transient" cases—in which the student's threat does not indicate a substantive intent to harm anyone—the incident can be resolved without significant disruption of the student's education. In more serious "substantive" cases, the threat assessment team develops a plan for addressing the threat and, even in these cases, the student usually returns to school. The distinction between transient and substantive cases is defined in Chapter 3.

Threat assessment also appears to be safer than other approaches because it involves a more comprehensive investigation of the threat. Unlike profiling, which places emphasis on individual student characteristics, threat assessment includes an investigation of the circumstances and origins of the threat, and it focuses on behaviors that indicate planning and preparation to carry out the threat (Cornell, 2004; Trump, 2000). Had Bob actually been planning to carry out his threat, a threat assessment would have made it more likely that the serious nature of the threat would be recognized. Simply expelling Bob under a zero tolerance policy would have done little to prevent Bob from carrying out the threat.

WHAT ARE THE LIMITATIONS OF THREAT ASSESSMENT?

Threat assessment is intended to be one part of a comprehensive school safety program. A comprehensive prevention program would include a strong school discipline policy, well-staffed counseling and psychological services, and school-based programs to help students resolve conflicts and overcome bullying (Osher, Dwyer, & Jackson, 2004). A safe school also requires adequate adult supervision of students throughout the school and at all school events (Trump, 1998). Threat assessment is not intended to prevent all forms of peer aggression or student violence, but it is a useful means of identifying certain potentially violent situations that can be investigated and prevented.

Our approach emphasizes the identification of threats expressed or communicated by students, as opposed to identifying students who seem dangerous to others but who have not expressed a threat to harm anyone. There are several reasons for this emphasis. One is that students do frequently express threats of violence—often without serious intention—and so guidelines on dealing with explicit threats would be helpful to school administrators. Another reason is that threats are more readily identified in a reliable manner, as opposed to a subjective judgment that someone seems dangerous. We believe that a focus on threats helps to avoid the pitfalls of profiling or stereotyping students, and that existing warning signs and lists of risk factors are too broad to be of much practical value to school administrators.

Nevertheless, there may be special circumstances in which a threat assessment approach is useful even in the absence of a specific threat. For example, if a student who has engaged in repeated acts of violence appears to be unusually angry and frustrated, it may be useful to conduct some elements of a threat assessment even if the student has not made an explicit threat. More generally, there are many circumstances in which school authorities may wish to conduct some form of inquiry or assessment that is not a formal threat assessment. Two examples are the assessment of a student who has made suicidal statements and inquiries concerning students who have engaged in disciplinary violations such as fights. Such inquiries might detect the presence of a threat and prompt the need for a threat assessment.

Threat assessment should be undertaken anytime a student threat is reported to school authorities. Therefore, school staff must understand the purpose and goals of threat assessment and be prepared to assist the school principal and threat assessment team in identifying and responding to threats. Threat assessment requires a shared commitment among school staff to work cooperatively and constructively to maintain school safety. Threat assessment also requires student cooperation, because many threats are observed only by students and must be reported to school authorities before they can be investigated. School staff must strive to engender a climate of trust and communication, so that students are willing to come forward when they are threatened or observe a threat being made. All students should be taught that seeking help from an adult in order to prevent an act of violence is not the same as "snitching" or "tattling" on a classmate in order to get the classmate in trouble.

> If the team determines a threat to be substantive—meaning that there is some risk that the student will carry out the threat—the focus becomes taking actions that will reduce risk, not measure it.

Threat assessment is not designed to *predict* violence but to identify potentially violent situations and resolve them. Therefore, threat assessment differs from other forms of risk assessment that aim to measure and quantify a student's degree of risk. From our threat assessment perspective, the risk that a student will carry out a threat varies continuously according to the changing situations and actions of everyone around the student. From this perspective, estimating the student's risk at a single point is not especially helpful. Once a threat is considered to be substantive—meaning that there is *some* risk that the student will carry out the threat— the threat assessment team is concerned with taking actions that will reduce risk, not measure it. This view requires a somewhat different perspective on risk than is generally found in the research literature, which is primarily concerned with validating measures of risk. From a threat assessment perspective, whenever there are findings that indicate a student is moving toward carrying out the threat—for example, the student has made repeated threats, has a detailed plan, and has acquired a weapon for the purpose of carrying out the plan—the team will increase its efforts to make sure the threat is not carried out.

Sometimes school psychologists ask why there is no provision for rating a student as low, medium, or high risk. Undoubtedly, some students are at higher risk than others, but the classification of students as low, medium, or high risk can be counterproductive to the goals of threat assessment, which are to *reduce* risk. Risk is not a static condition, and a student's risk rating is not a fixed quantity but is highly dependent on the context for the threat, including the unpredictable day-to-day changes in the student's life at home and at school. A student may be at low risk to carry out a threat when supervised at home or at school but at high risk if permitted to roam the streets at night with a group of peers. If threat assessment teams identify an individual student's reasons for making a threat and develop plans that address these reasons, the attempt to combine all possible contingencies into a single risk rating is not necessary.

This manual presents threat assessment *guidelines*, and guidelines are not a prescription or formula. Because threats can take many different forms and can occur in many different contexts, it is not possible to develop a definitive set of procedures or programmed answers to address every threat. This threat assessment procedure is not a threat assessment *test*. Threat assessment cannot be reduced to a single score or set of scores. Scoring systems necessarily rely on a discrete, closed set of variables, and they do not give adequate consideration to contextual factors and unique characteristics of the student, the setting and circumstance, and the intended victim. For these reasons, school authorities inevitably must rely on their professional judgment in making decisions about the seriousness of a threat and the appropriate course of action. The purpose of these guidelines is to provide a useful step-by-step framework for investigating a threat in a systematic manner, gathering relevant information,

---

KEY POINTS ABOUT THREAT ASSESSMENT

1. High-profile school shootings have generated an exaggerated perception of danger in schools.

2. Because of the fear of school violence, school administrators sometimes overreact to student behaviors that are not actually dangerous.

3. Profiles and warning signs can lead to false identification of students who are not truly dangerous.

4. Threat assessment offers a more flexible alternative to zero tolerance punishment because of the emphasis on understanding the *context* and *meaning* of the student's behavior.

Threat assessment emphasizes *investigating* and *resolving* threats in order to prevent violence, not quantifying risk.

considering the contextual factors associated with the threat, and taking reasonable action.

HOW WERE THESE GUIDELINES DEVELOPED?

The FBI report on school shootings (O'Toole, 2000) made a strong case that schools should take a threat assessment approach—rather than a profiling approach—to the identification of potentially violent students. The U.S. Secret Service and Department of Education report (Fein et al., 2002) made compelling arguments why schools should establish threat assessment teams and articulated key principles for conducting threat assessments. Unfortunately, the recommendations of these reports had not been systematically tested in schools. Would threat assessment work in schools? To address this gap between theory and practice, our group—the Virginia Youth Violence Project of the University of Virginia's Curry School of Education—decided to undertake the task of developing and field testing threat assessment guidelines for schools (Cornell, 2001). With the support of a three-year grant from the Jessie Ball duPont Fund, this work started in the spring of 2001 (Cornell, Sheras, Kaplan, McConville et al., 2004).

We began by collaborating with two public school divisions, Albemarle County and the City of Charlottesville, in central Virginia. These divisions serve urban, suburban, and rural areas in a single county that comprises 736 square miles and had a population of 129,000. The two school divisions had a combined enrollment of 16,273 students, of which 71% were Caucasian, 22% African American, and 7% other groups. Approximately 26% of the students were eligible for free or reduced-price meals. The school divisions included 35 schools: 4 high schools (grades 9–12), 6 middle schools (5 with grades 6–8; 1 with grades 7–8), 22 elementary schools, and 3 alternative schools.

We convened a work group consisting of school personnel who had experience dealing with student threats from multiple perspectives. Because student violence is such a sensitive topic, we were fortunate to have worked with both school divisions on previous projects. Each

school division sent an assistant superintendent, a principal, a school psychologist, and the supervisor of school resource officers. We also obtained input from school counselors and other educators, law enforcement officers, and local prosecutors.

We then established a multidisciplinary advisory group to review the guidelines as they were being developed. This advisory group consisted of state and national experts in education, law enforcement, and psychology. Serving in this group were the coordinator for the Office of Safe and Drug-Free Schools from the Virginia Department of Education (Arlene Cundiff), the director of the Virginia Center for School Safety in the Department of Criminal Justice Services (Donna Bowman), and the chair of the state Board of Juvenile Justice (Chip Harding). We were assisted by two leading scholars in violence prediction and forensic psychology (Kirk Heilbrun and John Monahan), and we received consultation from two members of the FBI's task force on school shootings (Mary Ellen O'Toole, and Terri Royster). This group proved to be an invaluable source of expertise and information.

We began by conducting telephone interviews with all of the school principals and psychologists in the two divisions. We asked them about the kinds of student threats that had come to their attention in the past year and what kinds of guidelines would have helped them respond. The principals reported that student threats to hurt someone were a relatively common event, but few threats were regarded as serious. The most significant concerns were (1) how to deal with minor, less serious threats in a fair and defensible manner; and (2) how to identify and respond to serious threats. Principals expressed concern that they relied mainly on intuition in making decisions about the seriousness of a student's risk for violence. Understandably, they were concerned about the consequences of failing to identify a truly violent student, and at the same time they did not want to overreact to a student comment or remark that was not a serious threat.

The school psychologists pointed out that they had little or no training in violence risk assessment and were uncomfortable being asked to make predictions about a student's likelihood of engaging in violent behavior. These observations were in line with studies of school psychology training (Furlong, Babinski, Poland, Munoz, & Boles, 1996) and reflect the lack of standards for such evaluations (Larson, Smith, & Furlong, 2001).

The concerns of both principals and psychologists made it clear that threat assessment required a set of written guidelines to assist staff in making determinations of the seriousness of a threat. It was recognized that an elaborate process of threat assessment would be burdensome to school authorities and that it would be necessary to design an efficient process to distinguish the less serious, commonplace threats from more serious threats, which would require a more labor-intensive response. It was decided that the school principals would conduct the initial evaluation of a threat and make a triage decision, either resolving a nonserious threat immediately or initiating a more comprehensive team assessment if the threat was serious. The work group meetings concluded with the preparation of the first version of *Guidelines for Responding to Student Threats of Violence*.

The next step was to train threat assessment teams in each of the 35 schools. Initially, for logistical reasons, there was a series of half-day training sessions with separate sessions for school principals, assistant principals and school resource officers, school psychologists, and school counselors. However, for some schools, training was provided to the entire team in one session, and it was soon apparent that this approach was more effective in helping teams to work together.

Training began with a PowerPoint® presentation covering the rationale for student threat assessment, a review of research on rates of school violence, and a summary of the findings and recommendations of the FBI study of school shootings (O'Toole, 2000). Then, the trainers presented a step-by-step review of the *Guidelines* decision tree (presented at the end of this chapter), illustrated with case examples of different types of threats. Next, there were sessions on legal issues and on the mental health assessment of students who made very serious substantive threats. The next stage was to have the participants meet in small groups to simulate their responses to a series of practice cases. The trainer presented participants with a hypothetical report of a threat and asked them to identify the first steps they would take in evaluating the threat. The trainer then presented more information about the threat as the group worked its way through the decision tree to resolution of the threat. After the groups completed three cases, they reconvened in full session to compare and discuss their work. Immediately after this discussion, participants completed a written quiz on their knowledge of the *Guidelines*.

CHAPTER 2

THE THREAT ASSESSMENT TEAM

WHY HAVE A THREAT ASSESSMENT TEAM AT EACH SCHOOL?

Each school should form its own threat assessment team rather than create a divisionwide team (Cornell, Sheras, Kaplan, Levy-Elkon, et al., 2004). While a single team would seem to be more efficient and require less training, there are a number of good arguments against this approach:

- School-based teams would make it easier for the assessment of student threats to be part of the regular school routine and make it more likely that threats would be reported and evaluated.

- Outside teams would have a slower response time, and threats require an immediate reaction.

- Threat assessment requires careful consideration of the environmental context for the threat, and an external team would be less familiar with students and personnel, as well as with recent school events and the overall school climate.

- There is potential for conflict between external teams and school personnel when they reach different opinions as to the seriousness of a threat.

- Because our threat assessment approach emphasizes follow-up contacts with the student and, in some cases, implementation of ongoing interventions to reduce the risk of violence, it would be preferable if the staff doing the threat assessment was on site.

WHO IS ON THE THREAT ASSESSMENT TEAM?

In the field-test schools, each team consisted of a principal or assistant principal, a school resource officer, a school psychologist, and a school counselor. However, schools differ in their staffing patterns, and some might need a different team structure. What is most important is to cover the team functions described in the following sections.

School principal or assistant principal. We decided that school principals should lead the threat assessment team because of their fundamental responsibility for student disciplinary matters and school safety. We recognized that it would be problematic for someone other than the school principal to be in a position of authority in making decisions about a student who had made a serious threat of violence. One exception is that in schools where the assistant principal is in charge of disciplinary matters, the principal might delegate the responsibility for team leadership to the assistant principal. As team leader, the school principal or assistant principal conducts the initial triage to determine the seriousness of the threat and, if the threat is serious, calls in the team. The school principal leads the team and makes final decisions about what to do in response to the student's threat. Other team members have responsibilities intended to provide the principal with information and recommendations to consider in making these decisions. We recommend that the team leader rely on multiple sources of information and consult with one or more team members in classifying threats and making important safety decisions.

School resource officer. Police officers with special training to work in schools are termed school resource officers, and their work has preventive as well as enforcement functions. The FBI (O'Toole, 2000) and U.S. Secret Service (Fein et al., 2002) reports recommend that schools place a school resource officer on every team. In schools where there are no resource officers, a police liaison officer could be identified from the local police department. Some school divisions employ school security officers who could undertake some of the functions and responsibilities of school resource officers. School administrators will need to evaluate the training and capabilities of their security officers and determine what role they could serve on the threat assessment team.

> Most important is that the law enforcement officer and the school principal understand how they can work together in different types of threat situations.

The school resource officer has several responsibilities on the team. First, the officer responds to emergencies or crisis situations in which there is an imminent risk of violence. In very serious cases, the officer has legal duties and responsibilities just as he or she would have if the threat situation took place outside of school. For example, a student wielding a weapon or a student who has injured someone is subject to arrest. In other cases, in which the risk of violence is not immediate, the officer might also have investigative responsibilities as part of his or her law enforcement role. For example, an officer might investigate a suspected bomb plot by obtaining a search warrant for a student's home. In such cases, the school resource officer does not act under the authority of the school principal but assumes independent responsibilities as a law enforcement officer.

In nonemergency situations, the school resource officer is a consultant on law enforcement matters. For example, the officer advises the team on matters of security or whether a student's behavior constituted a violation of law. Some states require that certain serious legal violations by students be reported to law enforcement authorities, which can be accomplished through the threat assessment team. Finally, schools can make use of their school resource officers for prevention purposes, consistent with the philosophy of community-oriented policing that seems well suited to school-based law enforcement (Atkinson, 1997). School resource officers can have a positive impact on the school climate by maintaining high visibility in the school; establishing positive, friendly relations with students; and taking an interest in school activities and events as another member of the school staff. They can adopt a problem-solving approach to crime prevention, identifying potentially volatile situations or brewing conflicts between students or groups of students before violent actions take place.

School psychologist. The school psychologist brings to the team expertise in psychological assessment and intervention that can be useful in responding to a student's aggressive behavior and in addressing the social and emotional difficulties that frequently underlie threatening behavior (Larson et al., 2001). In the case of a very serious substantive threat (defined in the following chapters), the school psychologist should conduct a mental health assessment of the student. This assessment, described in Chapter 5, is concerned initially with screening the student for mental health problems that demand immediate attention, such as psychosis or suicidality, and then with identifying the reasons why the student made the threat. With information from this assessment, the school psychologist will assist the team in developing a behavior plan or other interventions to reduce the risk of violence and respond to the student's educational needs.

School counselor. The school counselor also brings to the team expertise in working with

14

troubled students and helping them to resolve conflicts and problems in their relationships with others. The counselor should be someone who enjoys the trust and respect of students and who will be seen as a source of support and assistance in a difficult situation. The counselor might lead an effort to resolve a conflict or dispute within a group of students or provide individual counseling to deal with a student's anger or problems in making friends. In other cases, the counselor might identify programs or resources that could serve the student. After a behavior plan or other intervention plan has been developed, the school counselor can serve as the team member who then monitors the student's participation in the intervention plan and assesses its impact and continued effectiveness.

School social workers and other team members. Because of budget constraints, schools in the United States vary widely in their staffing patterns. In some school divisions, social workers can and should be enlisted as valuable members of the threat assessment team, particularly because of their traditional expertise in working with families, resolving conflicts, and helping students obtain needed assistance. Student assistance professionals, substance abuse counselors, school nurses, and other mental health professionals can also play an important role on a threat assessment team. In selecting team members, principals should give greater weight to the skill and experience of the individual staff member than the individual's specific discipline. Finally, teachers do not serve as regular members of the threat assessment team because their primary role is instruction and they have many other responsibilities. Nevertheless, there may be individual cases or circumstances in which teacher input to, or participation on, the threat assessment team would be useful.

HOW DO YOU USE THESE GUIDELINES?

Use the flowchart in *Figure 1* for guidance in responding to any student threat of violence. For each block of text on the flowchart, there

HOW CAN SCHOOLS PREPARE FOR A THREAT ASSESSMENT APPROACH?

All members of the school staff should be oriented to the threat assessment model so that they can identify and report threats and assist in any investigations and interventions that follow. School discipline policies should spell out the range of possible consequences for threatening behavior, and students should be educated about threats in schoolwide assemblies. Many students do not understand that sending a threatening letter or e-mail is a crime, or that scaring someone with a threat of physical violence is a form of assault. Parents should be given the same information and reassured that there are policies and procedures in place to deal with threats of violence.

Every teacher should spend time talking with students about the need to report threats of violence. Teachers should explain the difference between *snitching* on someone in order to get them into trouble and *seeking help* to prevent someone from being harmed. Teachers, counselors, and all other school staff should emphasize that they are willing and available to listen to any student's concerns.

are detailed instructions in the next two chapters. Principals do not need to conduct threat assessments for minor incidents, such as horseplay in the hallway or a routine incident in which a teacher admonishes a student to behave *and the incident is immediately resolved*. Threat assessments should be conducted when the incident is serious enough to generate an office referral or there is concern that a student may intend to harm someone in the future. A quick overview is provided here.

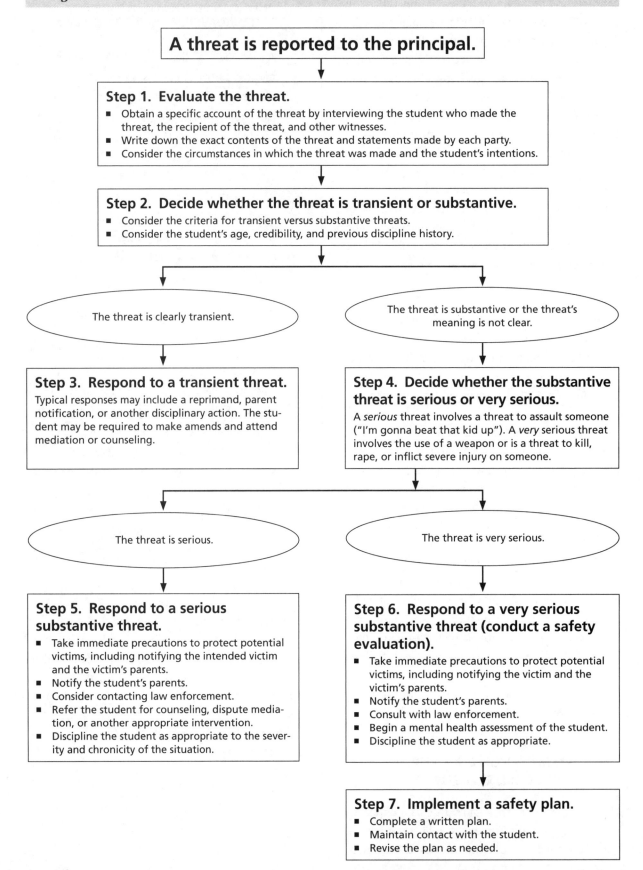

Figure 1. **Threat assessment decision tree**

A threat is reported to the principal.

Step 1. Evaluate the threat.
- Obtain a specific account of the threat by interviewing the student who made the threat, the recipient of the threat, and other witnesses.
- Write down the exact contents of the threat and statements made by each party.
- Consider the circumstances in which the threat was made and the student's intentions.

Step 2. Decide whether the threat is transient or substantive.
- Consider the criteria for transient versus substantive threats.
- Consider the student's age, credibility, and previous discipline history.

The threat is clearly transient.

The threat is substantive or the threat's meaning is not clear.

Step 3. Respond to a transient threat.
Typical responses may include a reprimand, parent notification, or another disciplinary action. The student may be required to make amends and attend mediation or counseling.

Step 4. Decide whether the substantive threat is serious or very serious.
A *serious* threat involves a threat to assault someone ("I'm gonna beat that kid up"). A *very* serious threat involves the use of a weapon or is a threat to kill, rape, or inflict severe injury on someone.

The threat is serious.

The threat is very serious.

Step 5. Respond to a serious substantive threat.
- Take immediate precautions to protect potential victims, including notifying the intended victim and the victim's parents.
- Notify the student's parents.
- Consider contacting law enforcement.
- Refer the student for counseling, dispute mediation, or another appropriate intervention.
- Discipline the student as appropriate to the severity and chronicity of the situation.

Step 6. Respond to a very serious substantive threat (conduct a safety evaluation).
- Take immediate precautions to protect potential victims, including notifying the victim and the victim's parents.
- Notify the student's parents.
- Consult with law enforcement.
- Begin a mental health assessment of the student.
- Discipline the student as appropriate.

Step 7. Implement a safety plan.
- Complete a written plan.
- Maintain contact with the student.
- Revise the plan as needed.

OVERVIEW OF THE SEVEN STEPS IN STUDENT THREAT ASSESSMENT

Step 1. Evaluate the threat. The principal investigates a reported threat by interviewing the student who made the threat and any witnesses to the threat. The principal considers the context and meaning of the threat, which are more important than the literal content of the threat.

Step 2. Decide whether the threat is transient or substantive. A *transient* threat is not a serious threat and can be easily resolved, but a *substantive* threat raises concern of potential injury to others. For transient threats, go to Step 3, and for substantive threats, skip to Step 4.

Step 3. Respond to a transient threat. If the threat is a transient threat, the principal may respond with a reprimand, parent notification, or other actions that are appropriate to the severity and chronicity of the situation. The incident is resolved, and no further action is needed.

Step 4. Decide whether the substantive threat is serious or very serious. If a threat is substantive, the principal must decide how serious the threat is and take appropriate action to protect potential victims. A threat to hit, assault, or beat up someone is serious, whereas a threat to kill, rape, use a weapon on, or severely injure someone is considered very serious. For serious threats, go to Step 5, and for very serious threats, skip to Step 6.

Step 5. Respond to a serious substantive threat. A serious substantive threat requires proactive, protective action to prevent violence, including notification of potential victims and other actions to address the conflict or problem that generated the threat. The response to a serious substantive threat is completed at this step.

Step 6. Respond to a very serious substantive threat (conduct a safety evaluation). A very serious substantive threat requires immediate protective action, including contact with law enforcement, followed by a comprehensive safety evaluation. The student is suspended from school pending completion of the safety evaluation, which includes a mental health assessment to determine referral and support needs.

Step 7. Implement a safety plan. The threat assessment team develops and implements a plan that is designed both to protect potential victims and to meet the student's educational needs. The plan includes a provision for monitoring the student and revising the plan as needed.

CHAPTER 3

BEGINNING THE THREAT ASSESSMENT

THE FIRST STEP

The first step in threat assessment is for the team leader—typically the principal or assistant principal—to interview the student who made the threat as well as witnesses to the threat. In some circumstances, it is desirable to interview one or more witnesses before interviewing the student, so that the interviewer is well informed and better prepared to evaluate the student's statements. The student interview is conducted in order to assess what the student intended by making the threatening statement or engaging in the threatening behavior, for the purpose of making a determination whether the threat is transient or substantive. The content or actual wording of the threat is less important than what the student meant and intended by making the threat.

In all cases, the team leader should strive to base decisions on information gathered from multiple sources, including one or more school staff members who have direct knowledge of the

---

Step 1. **Evaluate the threat.**

- Obtain a specific account of the threat by interviewing the student who made the threat, the recipient of the threat, and other witnesses.

- Write down the exact contents of the threat and statements made by each party.

- Consider the circumstances in which the threat was made and the student's intentions.

STUDENT INTERVIEW

Use these questions as the foundation for the interview. Modify and add to them as appropriate to the situation. Remember that the purpose of this interview is to evaluate the student's threat *in context*, so that you can determine what the student meant by the threat and whether the student has any intention of carrying out the threat. Do not promise confidentiality to the student, because in a potentially dangerous situation you cannot keep information confidential that is needed to protect others.

1. Do you know why I wanted to talk with you? Tell me.

2. What happened today when you were [place of incident]?

3. What exactly did you say? And what exactly did you do? (Write down the student's exact words.)

4. What did you mean when you said or did that?

5. How do you think [person who was threatened] feels about what you said or did? (See if the student believes it frightened or intimidated the person who was threatened.)

6. What was the reason you said or did that? (Find out if there is a prior conflict or history to this threat.)

7. What are you going to do now that you have made this threat? (Ask if the student intends to carry out the threat.)

WITNESS INTERVIEWS

Interview others who witnessed the threat, including the intended victim. Use these questions as the foundation for the interview. Modify and add to these questions as appropriate to the situation. Remember that the purpose of this interview is to evaluate the student's threat *in context,* so that you can determine what the student meant by the threat and whether the student has any intention of carrying out the threat.

1. What exactly happened today when you were [place of incident]?

2. What exactly did [student who made the threat] say (or do)? (Write down the student's exact words.)

3. What do you think he or she meant when saying (or doing) that?

4. How do you feel about what he or she said or did? (Gauge whether the person who observed or received the threat feels frightened or intimidated.) Are you concerned that he or she might actually do it?

5. Why did he or she say or do that? (Find out whether he or she knows of any prior conflict or history behind this threat.)

threat or relevant knowledge of the student. Team leaders are advised to consult with one or more team members in classifying threats and making important safety decisions. In complex cases, the team leader might enlist the direct involvement of other team members early in the assessment.

Interview as soon as possible. As soon as the threat has been reported, the team leader should interview the student who made the threat. Ideally, this interview should be conducted right away so that, if the threat is substantive, action can be taken promptly to prevent the threat

from being carried out. However, in some cases, it may not be possible to conduct an immediate interview—for example, if the threat was not reported until hours or days after it occurred or if the student is no longer on school premises. If it is not possible to interview the student right away, the team leader should gather information that is immediately available (perhaps by interviewing witnesses to the threat) and decide on a reasonable, provisional course of action that emphasizes the safety of anyone targeted by the threat. For example, the team leader might decide to warn a potential victim of a threat based on the reports of several witnesses that a student truly intended to assault a classmate later the same day. However, the team leader will interview the student at the first opportunity in order to conduct a more complete threat assessment. Suggested interview questions can be found in the Threat Assessment Documentation form in the Appendix.

Consider student and witness credibility. Experienced school personnel know that students do not always tell the truth and that students confronted with allegations of misbehavior may deny what they are accused of doing. It is also possible for students to be falsely accused. In ambiguous circumstances, there is no substitute for the judgment of the school staff member. Judgments of a student's credibility should be based on consideration of the student's demeanor and cooperativeness and on a history of any previous misbehavior or dishonesty. The team leader must be sure to compare the student's account with witness accounts, although the credibility of witnesses should also be considered. Unfortunately, there is no foolproof method for determining whether a student is being truthful;

Step 2. Decide whether the threat is transient or substantive.

- Consider the criteria for transient versus substantive threats.
- Consider the student's age, credibility, and previous discipline history.

even sophisticated polygraph machines are not considered reliable indicators of lying. When in doubt, the team should err on the side of safety and take those protective actions that would be appropriate if the threat were substantive.

WHAT ARE TRANSIENT THREATS?

Transient threats are defined as statements that do not express a lasting intent to harm someone. Transient threats either are intended as figures of speech or reflect feelings that dissipate in a short period when the student thinks about the meaning of what he or she has said. *All transient threats end in an apology or explanation that makes it clear the threat is over.*

It is important to realize that most threatening statements are not serious threats because the student has no substantive intention of carrying out the threat. A common example would be a statement made in jest or as a figure of speech. *The specific words of the threat are not as important as the context in which the threat is made.* The statement, "I'm gonna kill you," for instance, might be said over a chessboard, on the basketball court, or as a joke between friends. Ordinarily, everyone understands that the statement is not truly a threat and no one feels in danger. Students rarely report these kinds of threats to school staff, but occasionally someone overhears such a statement, misunderstands what is said, and reports it.

Another kind of transient threat occurs when a student says "I'm gonna kill you" in a moment of anger but does not really mean it and is willing to retract the statement when he or she calms down. Or, a student might make a threat as a tactic in an argument or as a means of intimidating someone ("Watch out or I'll take you out"). A linguist might want to make distinctions among these various types of transient threats; but, for practical purposes of threat assessment, all threats that do not convey a sustained intent to harm someone are grouped together as transient threats.

By definition, transient threats do not require protective action because there is no sustained intent to carry out the threat. Based on the field-test findings in 35 schools, approximately 70% (or more) of student threats will be transient threats. In contrast, substantive threats raise concern that someone is in danger of being harmed beyond the immediate incident. In these cases, there is a need to take some kind of action to protect a potential victim, such as separating the student from the potential victim, warning the victim, or contacting law enforcement.

TEN EXAMPLES OF TRANSIENT THREATS

1. "I'm gonna kill you"—said as a joke.

2. "I'm gonna kill you"—said in the heat of competition during a basketball game.

3. Two students use their fingers to "shoot" one another while playing cops and robbers.

4. "I'm gonna bust you up"—said in anger but then retracted after the student calms down.

5. "I could break you in half"—said to intimidate someone but retracted after the student calms down.

6. "I'll get you next time"—said after a fight but retracted after the two students reconcile.

7. "Watch out or I'll hurt you"—said to intimidate someone but retracted after the student calms down.

8. "I oughta shoot that teacher"—said in anger but retracted after the student calms down.

9. "There's a bomb in the building"— said in a phone call for the purpose of disrupting school, with there being no actual bomb.

10. A student is found with a pocket knife that he accidentally left in his backpack.

**TEN EXAMPLES OF
SUBSTANTIVE THREATS**

1. "I'm gonna kill you"—said with an intent to injure.

2. "I'm gonna kill you"—said while holding a weapon and not jokingly.

3. Two students exchange threats and then throw rocks at each other.

4. "I'm gonna bust you up"—said in anger and not retracted later.

5. "I could break you in half"—said in an intimidating manner, followed by stony silence.

6. "I'll get you next time"—said after a fight and the student refuses mediation.

7. "Watch out or I'll hurt you"—said by a student with a history of bullying.

8. "I oughta shoot that teacher"—said by a student who later denies making the statement.

9. "There's a bomb in the building"—said in a phone call made by a student who later is found to have bomb-making materials and plans at home.

10. A student who threatened to stab a classmate is found to have a pocket knife in his backpack.

WHAT ARE SUBSTANTIVE THREATS?

Substantive threats are defined as statements that express a continuing intent to harm someone. Substantive threats may express emotion like transient threats, but they also indicate a desire to harm someone that extends beyond the immediate incident or argument when the threat was made. In other words, a substantive threat has substance. If there is doubt or uncertainty about whether or not a threat is substantive, it should be treated as substantive and evaluated further. Again, we emphasize that the context and meaning of the threat are more important than the verbal content of the threat.

Transient threats and substantive threats can appear to be very similar. The same statement could be either transient or substantive, depending on the presence or absence of an enduring intent to harm someone. Often the team leader will determine that a threat is transient because the student retracts the threat and offers a convincing apology. Or, a threat may be transient because the team leader is able to facilitate resolution of the disagreement that sparked the threat so that both parties are no longer in conflict. In contrast, *a threat not retracted or resolved should be considered substantive.*

Presumptive indicators. There are some presumptive indicators of a substantive threat. This means that, if any of these factors are present, the team leader should presume that the

**PRESUMPTIVE INDICATORS OF A
SUBSTANTIVE THREAT**

- The threat contains specific, plausible details. ("I am going to shoot Mr. Smith with my shotgun," rather than "I am going to set off an atomic bomb" or "I'll get you for that.")

- The threat has been repeated over time or the student has told multiple parties of the threat.

- The threat is reported to others as a plan, or there are suggestions that violent action has been planned. ("Wait and see what happens next Tuesday in the cafeteria!")

- There are accomplices, or the student has sought out accomplices, in order to carry out the threat.

- The student has invited peers to observe the threat being carried out. ("Come and watch.")

- There is physical evidence of intent to carry out the threat. Such evidence could include written plans, lists of victims, drawings, weapons, bomb materials, or literature encouraging or describing how to carry out acts of violence.

student has made a substantive threat unless there is clear and convincing evidence to the contrary. Therefore, these indicators are presumptive but not conclusive.

Factors to consider in distinguishing between transient and substantive threats.

Consider the age, credibility, and discipline record of the student who made the threat. An older student is considered more likely to make a substantive threat than a younger student. A student who acknowledges his or her inappropriate behavior and gives a credible denial of intent to actually harm someone is less likely to have made a substantive threat than a student who doesn't acknowledge his or her behavior. Judge credibility based on the student's presentation of what happened as well as on all other information you have about this student, including personal knowledge. Be sure to compare the student's account with accounts of other witnesses to identify any discrepancies or omissions. A student with a discipline record that indicates previous aggressive behavior, dishonesty, or both is considered more likely to make a substantive threat than a student whose discipline record is more favorable. If there is significant doubt whether a threat is transient or substantive, treat the threat as substantive.

HOW DO YOU DECIDE WHETHER A THREAT IS TRANSIENT?

A threat is transient if it can be quickly and easily resolved (see *Figure 2*). If a threat cannot be quickly and easily resolved, it should be considered substantive. If there is uncertainty about whether a threat is transient or substantive, the best approach is to treat the threat as substantive.

Figure 2. **Responding to transient threats**

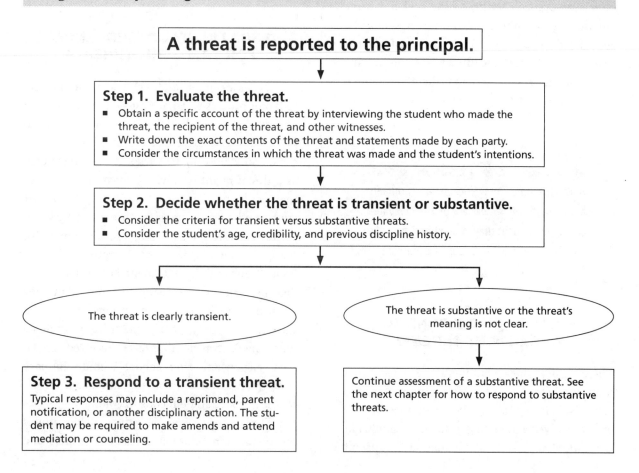

A threat is reported to the principal.

Step 1. Evaluate the threat.
- Obtain a specific account of the threat by interviewing the student who made the threat, the recipient of the threat, and other witnesses.
- Write down the exact contents of the threat and statements made by each party.
- Consider the circumstances in which the threat was made and the student's intentions.

Step 2. Decide whether the threat is transient or substantive.
- Consider the criteria for transient versus substantive threats.
- Consider the student's age, credibility, and previous discipline history.

The threat is clearly transient.

The threat is substantive or the threat's meaning is not clear.

Step 3. Respond to a transient threat.
Typical responses may include a reprimand, parent notification, or another disciplinary action. The student may be required to make amends and attend mediation or counseling.

Continue assessment of a substantive threat. See the next chapter for how to respond to substantive threats.

Transient threats that are jokes or figures of speech can be identified fairly easily from the context of the threat. Information from the student and witnesses should indicate that the threatening statement was intended as humor, metaphor, or perhaps hyperbole, but that it did not indicate intent to carry out the threatened act. Occasionally, a threat may be reported because someone misunderstood or misinterpreted a student's threatening statement, but the student should be able to clarify what he or she meant.

Transient threats that are expressions of anger or frustration are somewhat more difficult to identify than transient threats that are jokes or figures of speech; nevertheless, the team leader (usually the principal or assistant principal) should be able to conclude that the threat has been resolved and no longer exists, based on the student's response to the threat assessment. The student who makes a transient threat in a moment of anger or frustration should be able to calm down and retract the threat. The student should be willing to apologize for the threat and offer reassurance that he or she will not carry out the threat. Otherwise, the threat should be considered substantive. The team leader must be comfortable that the threat is resolved; this means the leader must conclude that the student's apology is genuine.

Step 3. Respond to a transient threat.
Typical responses may include a reprimand, parent notification, or another disciplinary action. The student may be required to make amends and attend mediation or counseling.

HOW DO YOU RESPOND TO A TRANSIENT THREAT?

There is no single, automatic response to a transient threat. The response to a transient threat depends on the context of the threat, whether the threat involved a disciplinary violation, and what is required to resolve the situation. Transient threats that represent poor attempts at humor or figures of speech may not require a response beyond a reprimand or corrective instruction. However, if a student repeatedly makes inappropriate statements that are disruptive or annoying to others, a more elaborate response may be indicated.

Transient threats made in anger are more complex than such threats made in an attempt at humor. Angry statements that do not express genuine intent to harm someone are nevertheless inappropriate. The student should receive counseling and discipline in proportion to the nature of the statement and its effect on others. The student's recognition that the statement was inappropriate and willingness to make amends or apologize should be considered.

A transient threat often indicates a conflict or dispute between the student and the threat recipient. In such cases, there should be a dispute resolution effort, such as referral to conflict mediation or some other counseling designed to resolve the underlying problem.

DISCIPLINARY CONSEQUENCES FOR TRANSIENT THREATS

Threat assessment and school discipline are separate processes. Some transient threats merit little in the way of disciplinary consequences and others merit severe consequences. For example, a student whose figure of speech is interpreted as a threat might be advised not to use language that could be construed as a threat. Another student who used a transient threat as a means of getting attention in class might be disciplined for inappropriate language or disruptive behavior. Some transient threats might be so disruptive, disrespectful, or distressing to others that they merit more serious disciplinary consequences. In the field-test study, nearly one third of students who made transient threats received short-term suspensions from school. The disciplinary consequences for a threat should depend largely on the school's student code of conduct.

The classic example that demonstrates the distinction between threat assessment and discipline is a false bomb threat. A student who calls in a false bomb threat is making a transient threat—that is, the threat is intended as a joke or prank or perhaps as an attempt to intimidate or disrupt the school, but it does not reflect a true intent to blow up the school. Nevertheless, bomb threats are serious legal violations, and the student could be arrested and charged with a crime. School authorities might discipline the student with a long-term suspension or expulsion.

It is important to distinguish between the *seriousness of a threat* and the *seriousness of a discipline violation*. For example, a student might become angry at a teacher and make a threatening statement, but later retract the threat and apologize. Even though the threat is found to be transient, threatening a teacher might be regarded as a serious *disciplinary* violation meriting serious consequences. Schools should be careful not to classify a threat as substantive because the behavior constitutes a serious discipline violation. *Severe disciplinary consequences are appropriate in response to some transient threats if the behavior is sufficiently disruptive or disrespectful.*

Finally, a threat might occur at the same time as another, more serious disciplinary violation. For example, a student might be involved in a fight and also make an angry statement after the fight is broken up. In such a case, the student might receive serious disciplinary consequences for the fight and less serious consequences for the transient threat.

IS THERE A DUTY TO TAKE PROTECTIVE ACTION AFTER A TRANSIENT THREAT?

No. By definition, a transient threat does not involve an enduring intent to harm someone. Protective action is taken only if the threat is substantive. If the leader of the threat assessment team judges that there is some risk that the student will carry out the threat, even after the student has apologized and retracted the threat, then the threat should be considered substantive. A substantive threat always requires some form of protective action.

Although a threat may be transient, it may still indicate a conflict or problem that merits attention. For example, if a transient threat was made because a student was angry or upset with someone, there should be some effort made to resolve the underlying conflict or problem that stimulated the threat. This preventive action is not an attempt to protect someone from the threat; rather, it is designed to prevent the conflict or problem from generating a new threat or incident.

> Do not classify a threat as substantive merely because the behavior constitutes a serious discipline violation.

IF A STUDENT IS THREATENED, SHOULD I CONTACT THE STUDENT'S PARENTS?

Yes. Although many school administrators are reluctant to contact the parents of a student who has been threatened, most parents would insist on being informed and would complain if they were not. If a threat is transient, there is no duty to warn the parents as a protective action, but the school should contact the parents in order to offer reassurances that the threat has been addressed and their child is not in danger from the threat. Some school administrators may hope that the parents never hear of the threat, but this is a gamble that may make things worse. Parents who are not informed that their child was threatened have good reason to be upset with the school. Failure to notify parents that their child was threatened can create a firestorm of parental criticism.

In contacting the parents of a student who was threatened, the school administrator should be sensitive to the parents' fears and concerns. Parents should be informed how the threat was investigated, what was determined, how the threat was resolved, and what steps are being taken to address the underlying problem that stimulated the threat. There is more information on this issue in Chapter 6. Confidentiality issues are covered in Chapter 7.

Below are three case examples of transient threats.

Transient play shooting. *Two elementary school students in the cafeteria pointed their fingers at each other, pretending to shoot guns. They then turned and shot at a teacher's aide.*

Response. The principal interviewed the students and the classroom teacher. The teacher reported that the students are sometimes boisterous in class but that they have not threatened or assaulted others. The students did not know the teacher's aide and had no history of conflict with her. The principal judged that the students were playing and did not intend to frighten or intimidate the teacher's aide. The principal concluded that this was a transient threat that could be handled without further investigation. The principal admonished the students and explained to them that their behavior was inappropriate. The students were contrite and apologized to the teacher's aide.

Transient indirect bomb threat. *A second grade student was sent to the office for repeatedly misbehaving in class. On the way out of the classroom, he muttered, "I oughta blow this place up." Several students heard him and reported the statement to the teacher, who in turn contacted the principal.*

Response. The principal interviewed the student, who admitted making the statement but said he made the statement only because he was mad. The principal contacted the boy's mother, who said her son has not talked about bombs and does not have access to materials to make a bomb. The teacher interviewed the students who heard the statement. These witnesses had not heard the student make statements about using bombs before this incident. Although the boy had misbehaved repeatedly in class, he had not been aggressive or threatening with others. The principal decided this statement was expressive rather than substantive. The parents were called in for a meeting about the boy's repeated misbehavior and his threatening statement. The boy was seen by the school counselor to talk about his feelings about school. The boy was given two days of in-school suspension.

Transient threat during a fight. *Two middle school boys were fighting in the hallway. After they were separated by two teachers, one boy shouted, "I'm gonna kill you for that."*

Response. The principal interviewed the student, who admitted making the statement but said he made the statement because he was mad. He explained what the other student had done to offend him and how the fight started. The boy denied that he would attempt to kill the other student or that he had any plans to do so. The boy was apologetic and agreed to meet with the other student and try to resolve their conflict. The principal was familiar with both boys and knew their discipline records. The principal consulted with the teachers for any additional information about the conflict between them and concluded that the threat was a transient threat. Although the threat was judged to be a transient threat, the principal decided that an appropriate consequence for the incident was to suspend both boys for fighting. Their parents were contacted, and the entire situation, including the threatening statement, was reviewed. The school resource officer met with each boy and pointed out the legal consequences that could follow from fighting and threatening behavior. The boys attended a mediation session to resolve their conflict. After the mediation session, the school counselor interviewed each boy to assess whether the conflict had been resolved. The boys were encouraged to contact the school counselor if there was renewed conflict.

CHAPTER 4

RESPONDING TO SUBSTANTIVE THREATS

Any threat that cannot be readily identified as transient should be regarded as substantive. The most important distinction between a transient and a substantive threat is that the team must take protective action so that a substantive threat is not carried out. The degree of protective action taken depends on the seriousness of the threat. Because all substantive threats by definition are serious threats, our guidelines distinguish between threats that are *serious* and those that are *very serious* (see *Figure 3*).

Figure 3. **Responding to substantive threats**

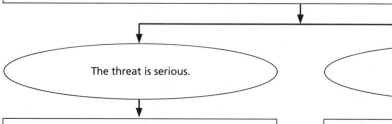

The threat is substantive or the meaning of the threat is not clear.

Step 4. Decide whether the substantive threat is serious or very serious.
A *serious* threat involves a threat to assault someone ("I'm gonna beat that kid up"). A *very* serious threat involves the use of a weapon or is a threat to kill, rape, or inflict severe injury on someone.

The threat is serious.

The threat is very serious.

Step 5. Respond to a serious substantive threat.
- Take immediate precautions to protect potential victims, including notifying the intended victim and the victim's parents.
- Notify the student's parents.
- Consider contacting law enforcement.
- Refer the student for counseling, dispute mediation, or another appropriate intervention.
- Discipline the student as appropriate to the severity and chronicity of the situation.

Step 6. Respond to a very serious substantive threat (conduct a safety evaluation).
- Take immediate precautions to protect potential victims, including notifying the victim and the victim's parents.
- Notify the student's parents.
- Consult with law enforcement.
- Begin a mental health assessment of the student.
- Discipline the student as appropriate.

Step 7. Implement a safety plan.
- Complete a written plan.
- Maintain contact with the student.
- Revise the plan as needed.

Step 4. Decide whether the substantive threat is serious or very serious. A *serious* threat involves a threat to assault someone ("I'm gonna beat that kid up"). A *very serious* threat involves the use of a weapon or is a threat to kill, rape, or inflict severe injury on someone.

A substantive threat that involves using a weapon such as a firearm or a knife will be classified as very serious because of the potential for severe injury. Severe injury means that the victim would require immediate medical treatment, such as for a stabbing wound, gunshot wound, or broken limb. Even though it is possible that a person could sustain a severe injury from any kind of assault, for threat assessment purposes the only substantive threats to be classified as *very serious* are those that involve a weapon or a threat to kill, rape, or sexually assault someone. The distinction between a serious and a very serious substantive threat is comparable to the distinction between a misdemeanor assault and a felonious assault.

RESPONDING TO A SERIOUS SUBSTANTIVE THREAT

A serious substantive threat usually involves a fight or a threat to hit someone or to beat someone up without the use of a weapon. The full team need not be involved in a serious substantive threat. Depending upon the circumstances of the threat, the team leader will choose which team members are needed to assist in preventing the threat from being carried out and then to plan an intervention designed to remedy the conflict or problem that led to the threat. The team leader will document the threat assessment, including protective actions, on the Threat Assessment Documentation form in the Appendix.

A. *Take immediate precautions to protect potential victims.* In responding to a serious substantive threat, the team leader should take appropriate precautions to protect

EXAMPLES OF SERIOUS AND VERY SERIOUS SUBSTANTIVE THREATS

Serious

- A student threatens to hit or strike a classmate with his fist.
- A student says she is going to beat someone up after school.
- A student sends a note saying, "I'm going to punch you out tomorrow at the bus stop."
- A student tells a classmate, "Rob is gonna get jumped at lunchtime."
- Two students say, "We're gonna get him alone and rough him up today."

Very Serious

- A student tells several classmates that he has prepared a hit list of people whom he intends to shoot on the following Monday.
- A student is found to have bomb-making materials in his home and a map of the school with marked locations for placing bombs.
- A student says that he is tired of being bullied on the school bus and plans to bring a gun to defend himself.
- A student brings a baseball bat to school and threatens to use it to beat up another student.
- A male student has been stalking a female student and threatened to sexually assault her.
- A student tells a classmate, "I'm gonna strangle him until he's dead."
- A student tells a classmate, "I'm gonna let the air out of him today" (meaning stab him with a knife).

potential victims. The nature of these precautions depends on the circumstances of the threat, as well as any information

> ### Step 5. Respond to a serious substantive threat.
>
> - Take immediate precautions to protect potential victims, including notifying the intended victim and the victim's parents.
> - Notify the student's parents.
> - Consider contacting law enforcement.
> - Refer the student for counseling, dispute mediation, or another appropriate intervention.
> - Discipline the student as appropriate to the severity and chronicity of the situation.

indicating how soon and where the threat might be carried out. Typical immediate protective actions include:

- Cautioning the student who made the threat about the consequences of carrying it out;

- Providing direct supervision so that the student cannot carry out the threat while at school;

- Contacting the student's parents to assume responsibility for supervising the student after he or she is returned to parental control (usually the parents will be required to come for the student so that he or she will not be released from school without parental supervision).

Sometimes school authorities cannot provide immediate supervision because the student is at large in the school or is not at school. Under these circumstances, school authorities must make an immediate effort to locate the student and place him or her under direct supervision or take appropriate steps if the student cannot be found. For example, school authorities might contact the intended victim or victims of the threat, warn them of the threat, and take prudent steps to protect them, such as summoning

the school resource officer and notifying teachers.

The level of supervision provided to the student should be consistent with the nature and seriousness of the threat. For example, a student who threatens to beat up a classmate and seems intensely angry and ready to carry out the threat immediately should be kept in an office or classroom under continuous adult supervision. If the school has a school resource officer, the officer should meet with the student. More often, however, a student will calm down and agree not to have any contact with the classmate and, under these conditions, may return to class. As a precaution, the student might be kept from a class attended by that classmate, and the student might be required to report to the office prior to school dismissal, rather than being released to ride the same bus as the classmate.

1. **Notify the intended victim and his or her parents.** In most cases, the intended victim is present when the threat is made; however, in some cases the student makes the threat to a third party or anonymously (e.g., by letter), in which case school authorities should notify the intended victim that a threat was made. Victims should be fully informed about the content of the threat and the identity of the student who made the threat. If the victim of the threat is a student, then the student's parents should be notified as well.

   Victims and their parents often feel angry in response to a threat, so it may be appropriate to reassure them that the school is taking action on their behalf and to caution them not to retaliate. Sometimes school authorities are reluctant to notify a victim and his or her parents because of a concern that they might take aggressive action against the student or the student's family. Nevertheless, the school has an obligation to notify the victim's

31

parents, who would be even angrier at the school if not notified. It seems unlikely that school authorities could prevent a victim or a victim's parents from ever finding out that a threat has taken place. On the contrary, school authorities should make a concerted effort to establish a trusting relationship with parents of victims by dealing with them in an open and straightforward manner and by reassuring them that strong actions are being taken, in concert with law enforcement, to deal with the threat. Additional information on confidentiality and parent notification issues is found in Chapter 7.

2. **Notify the parents of the student who made the threat.** Parents should be notified anytime a student makes a violent threat. This notification is both a disciplinary response and a protective action, because the parents are expected to assume responsibility for supervising their child once he or she has left school.

The parents should be informed of the nature of the student's threat, who was threatened, and the consequences for the student if he or she carries out the threat. School authorities should communicate to the parents that they will try to identify and resolve whatever problems or circumstances precipitated the threat and attempt to help the student respond in a more constructive and adaptive manner. In this context, they should attempt to enlist parental support and assistance in preventing the student from carrying out the threat.

Parents need not be told who reported the threat, particularly if there is concern for protecting that person's anonymity. However, parents must be assured that the information regarding the threat is reliable. Sometimes a student will deny making a threat, and the parents will challenge the validity of the report. In such circumstances, it is particularly important that the team leader has made careful notes of what was reported by each witness, which can be used to speak authoritatively about the threat incident. If the team leader has significant uncertainty about whether the threat actually occurred, he or she may decide to take protective action as a precautionary measure, suspending the decision to discipline the student until further investigation indicates clearer evidence of a violation.

B. *Consider contacting law enforcement.* If the school has an on-site school resource officer, it would be best to involve the officer on a routine basis in serious substantive threats as part of his or her regular responsibilities in monitoring and supervising student behavior. If an officer is not readily available to the school, the decision to contact law enforcement is influenced primarily by the nature of the threat and the need for assistance in taking protective action. Administrators who are experienced in dealing with students who make threats to hit or beat up someone may feel that they can manage many incidents without law enforcement assistance.

C. *Refer the student for counseling, dispute mediation, or another appropriate intervention.* After taking immediate protective action and contacting all appropriate parties, the team will want to consider interventions that would remedy the underlying conflict that led to the threat. These interventions are also intended to reduce the threat of violence but may take longer to implement and take effect. Typically, the first step is to engage the student in individual counseling to understand the reasons why the threat was made and to help the student identify more acceptable ways to communicate or seek help for a problem. If there is a dispute or argument underlying the threat, some form of dispute mediation is usually a good option. However, mediation requires that both parties are willing to participate, and mediation is not always appropriate, particularly in bully–victim conflicts in which the parties do not have equal strength or status in negotiation. Consider the intervention strategies described in Chapter 8.

D. *Discipline the student as appropriate to the severity and chronicity of the situation.* Threat assessment and school discipline are separate processes, so school authorities are free to apply their own disciplinary standards to threat incidents. A substantive threat to harm someone likely merits some disciplinary response because it is an aggressive act and disruptive to the learning environment. However, a threat to hit someone is less severe than actually hitting someone.

In some cases, a threat may occur at the same time as another, more serious disciplinary violation. For example, after being in a fight with a classmate, a student might threaten to continue the fight later on. In this case, the student might receive serious disciplinary consequences for the fight and additional consequences for the threat.

Step 6. Respond to a very serious substantive threat (conduct a safety evaluation).

- Take immediate precautions to protect potential victims, including notifying the victim and the victim's parents.
- Notify the student's parents.
- Consult with law enforcement.
- Begin a mental health assessment of the student.
- Discipline the student as appropriate.

RESPONDING TO A VERY SERIOUS SUBSTANTIVE THREAT

The full threat assessment team should be involved in a very serious substantive threat. The team's investigation of the threat is termed a "safety evaluation" to distinguish it from a special education evaluation, child study meeting, manifestation determination, or other form of evaluation. The purpose of the safety evaluation is to identify and carry out any actions necessary to reduce the risk of violence, as well as to gather information relevant to whether the student can return to school.

A. *Take immediate precautions to protect potential victims.* The classification of a *very serious substantive threat* is reserved for only the most serious and dangerous threat situations. It is expected that a school would have few or no cases of very serious substantive threats each year. Undoubtedly, the superintendent's office would expect to be advised of any very serious substantive threats.

All of the precautions taken for a serious substantive threat should be considered in the case of a very serious substantive threat. These precautions include supervising the student who made the threat, contacting the student's parents, and consulting with the team's law enforcement officer. In addition, the team should take steps to determine whether the student has access to a weapon such as a gun or knife, even if the threat does not specify use of a weapon ("I'm going to kill him").

1. **Notify the intended victim and his or her parents.** Notification is required if there is an identifiable victim or small group of identifiable victims. In these cases, school authorities should contact each victim and, if the victim is a minor, also contact the parents. The instructions for notifying victims of serious substantive threats apply here too.

Even if the victim is aware of the threat, it would be appropriate to contact the victim and convey concern that the threat is very serious. In most cases, this contact occurs in the course of investigating the threat, but there may be situations where the intended victim is not present or does not recognize the seriousness of the threat.

If the threat is aimed at a broad group (e.g., members of the football team or all students in the school), then school authorities, in consultation with law enforcement, should decide on an appropriate and timely way of notifying members of the group. The decision to notify a threatened group should be based first on consideration of the danger faced by members of the group. For example, if the student who made the threat is in custody, there is not an urgent need to contact group members. Nevertheless, school authorities should advise group members of the presence of the threat and explain the steps taken to ensure their safety. This communication might take place in the form of phone calls or a general letter, and in some cases it would be appropriate to follow up with a general meeting for concerned parties. Communications should emphasize engaging victim and parent cooperation and discouraging provocative responses to the student who made the threat.

When a very serious substantive threat has become a matter of general knowledge in the school or community, it may be a source of distress or disruption. Therefore, in these situations it would be appropriate to share some general information about the situation with the student body or the community as a whole. See Chapter 7 for more information on parent notification and the issue of confidentiality.

2. **Notify the parents of the student who made the threat.** Students who have made very serious substantive threats are subject to either arrest by law enforcement or immediate suspension from school. In either case, school authorities should notify the student's parents as soon as possible. The parent notification instructions for serious substantive threats apply here as well. Again, it is particularly important to enlist parental support and assistance in preventing the student from carrying out the threat.

B. *Consult with law enforcement.* It is a good idea to keep the school resource officer (SRO) advised of any student threat, but, if a student makes a very serious substantive threat, the SRO should be contacted immediately. The SRO can provide advice on the seriousness of the situation, initiate a law enforcement investigation of the threat, and, in appropriate circumstances, take protective action. If an SRO is not available, the principal should contact another law enforcement officer (e.g., the SRO supervisor for the school division). In an emergency situation, the principal should call 911 and follow the school's crisis response plan. Throughout the threat assessment process, school authorities should remain in close communication with law enforcement and obtain law enforcement advice and recommendations.

C. *Begin a mental health assessment of the student.* The mental health assessment should be conducted by the school psychologist or another mental health professional on the school staff. The term "mental health assessment" is used in a generic sense to refer to the kind of assessment ordinarily undertaken by a school psychologist or other mental health professional conducting an inquiry into the mental health status of a student for the purpose of determining the student's referral and support needs. The school psychologist or other mental health professional should conduct this assessment within the scope of local laws and regulations governing professional practice.

The mental health assessment is described in detail in Chapter 5 and should include a short written report. This assessment is an important part of the team's safety evaluation, but the mental health professional should not assume responsibility for the complete safety evaluation.

In the event of a very serious substantive threat, the principal should immediately notify the school psychologist or another mental health professional designated to conduct the mental health assessment. If possible, the mental health professional should begin the assessment on the day that the threat becomes known to the principal. The purpose of an immediate interview is to assess the student's emotional state and determine whether there are urgent mental health needs (e.g., suicide risk, psychosis, rage) that should be addressed. After the first day, the mental health professional should obtain parent permission to conduct further assessment of the student. At this point, the primary purpose of the assessment is to gather information about the student's motives in making the threat, as well as to determine the presence of risk or protective factors, so that the team can identify strategies for reducing the risk of violence through an effective intervention plan (e.g., resolving a peer dispute or identifying a bully–victim relationship).

In some circumstances, it may not be possible to conduct a complete mental health assessment because the student has been arrested or is not coming back to school. In other cases, a mental health assessment may be supplemented or shortened by the availability of other sources of information, such as a recent evaluation for special education services. However, even with ample information from other sources, it is important to assess the student's current mental state and the circumstances surrounding the threat. In most cases, a prior evaluation for special education purposes does not address the topics relevant to violence, which are described in Chapter 5.

If the parent declines permission for the mental health assessment, ask about the basis of his or her objection and see whether it is possible to satisfy these concerns. In most cases, a mental health assessment is essential to determining whether it is safe for the student to return to school. Parents should be advised that failure to cooperate with the safety evaluation prevents school authorities from preparing a plan for the student to return to school or to continue his or her education in an alternative setting. School administrators are advised to consider local legal requirements and regulations in these circumstances.

D. *Discipline the student as appropriate.* The threat assessment team should meet for the purpose of sharing information, analyzing the student's threat behavior, and determining appropriate steps to maintain safety. The six principles of threat assessment presented in Chapter 1 (derived from Vossekuil et al., 2002) should guide this process. In brief, they are:

1. **Prevention is possible.** Targeted violence is not a spontaneous, unpredictable event but is the result of a deliberate and detectable process and is often preceded by days or weeks of thought and planning.

2. **Consider the context.** In the case of very serious substantive threats, investigate whether there are factors such as peer influences, gang rivalries, or recent incidents that encourage violence or discourage more appropriate ways of resolving problems or seeking help.

3. **Adopt an investigative mind-set.** Avoid conjecture and speculation. Be skeptical. Focus on reliable evidence and verify all claimed facts about the situation.

4. **Rely on facts, not profiles.** Conclusions must be based on objective

facts and behaviors rather than inferred traits or characteristics of the student making the threat.

5. **Gather information from multiple sources.** Gather information from students, parents, teachers, counselors, and other school personnel, as well as from law enforcement, mental health agencies, and other sources in the community.

6. **Assess how the student poses a threat.** Threat assessment is ultimately concerned with whether the student *poses* a threat, not whether the student has *made* a threat. Is the student engaged in planning and preparation to carry out the threat?

Step 7. Implement a safety plan.

- Complete a written plan.
- Maintain contact with the student.
- Revise the plan as needed.

IMPLEMENT A SAFETY PLAN

The purpose of the safety evaluation is to develop and implement a safety plan that has three main objectives: (1) to resolve the threat of violence so as to maintain the safety of any potential victims; (2) to address any factors in the school environment (such as bullying or peer conflict) that played a contributory role in the threat situation; and (3) to return the student to school or an alternative educational program.

A. *Complete a written plan.* The threat assessment team should meet to share information and develop a common understanding of the threat. The team's plan should include the immediate steps taken to prevent the threat from being carried out and a plan for further action. Ordinarily these actions would include conditions under which the student

could return to school, or continue in an alternative educational setting, and any interventions such as counseling or mediation that are deemed appropriate. The results of this meeting will be summarized in a short Safety Evaluation Report, which should be placed in a confidential section of the student's file. A template for this report and a case example are presented in the Appendix. A written plan is recommended for three reasons: (1) to establish clearly what has been decided and how the plan will be carried out; (2) to provide adequate legal record of a responsible and appropriate response to the threat; and (3) to provide information for school staff in the event of another incident or threatening situation in another grade or a different school.

B. *Maintain contact with the student.* Every safety plan should include provision for follow-up contact with the student to verify that the plan has been successfully implemented to meet the school's safety needs and the needs of the student. For example, if the student's threat was a reaction to bullying by another student, there will be regular contact with the student to assess whether any bullying has occurred. The safety plan will specify the individual or individuals responsible for follow-up contacts.

C. *Revise the plan as needed.* The team should continue to monitor the situation after the student returns to school and make any changes in the plan that seem reasonable to maintain safety. Safety plans should include provision for a follow-up review of the student's behavior and attitude toward the intended victim of the threat. If there is indication that the student is still at risk to carry out the threat, the plan should be revised accordingly.

SAFETY EVALUATION REPORT

This brief report is prepared by the principal or designee when a student makes a threat of violence that is determined to be a very serious substantive threat. The report describes the results of the school's safety evaluation and should be kept in the confidential section of the student's file. The report is completed within 30 days of learning about the threat and should include the following information.

Identifying information. Give the student's name, grade, gender, and any other relevant identifying information. List all members of the threat assessment team.

Threat description. Specify all information relevant to the threat, including where and when the threat occurred, identifying information for the intended victim or recipient of the threat, names of witnesses, and a description of the threat in context.

Threat response. This section describes the school's immediate response to the threat, documenting that the school followed these guidelines. Because this report is prepared when the threat is judged to be a very serious substantive threat, the report should specify the following dates of action: (1) when the police were notified; (2) when the student's parents or guardians were notified; (3) when the intended victim (and the parents, if applicable) was notified; and (4) when

the student received a mental health assessment. This section should also indicate any immediate actions taken to ensure safety, such as conducting a search for weapons or evacuating the school in response to a bomb threat, as well as the dates when the student was suspended, pending determination of safety.

Action plan. This section describes the plan of action resulting from the school's safety evaluation. The safety evaluation states the conditions under which the student may return to school, such as participation in counseling, and a timetable for follow-up contacts with the student and parents. The plan should identify a person who will verify that plan recommendations are being followed. This section will note any specific risk factors that should be monitored, such as the resolution of a bullying problem. It should include any other consequences for the student, such as court involvement, expulsion, or placement in an alternative educational setting.

If the student participates in special education services, this section should cite how the student's disability was considered and what, if any, changes to the student's individualized education program (IEP) were recommended. Changes to the IEP are always made by the IEP team.

A case example of a Safety Evaluation Report is presented on the following page.

Safety Evaluation Report—Case Example   CONFIDENTIAL

Student's name John Smith   Grade 7   (Male)/ Female

Team members Annette Thomas, Ed.D., principal; Julia Bronson, Ed.S., school psychologist;

Officer James Johnson, school resource officer; Grant Jones, school counselor

Date of threat 11/20   Date learned of threat (if different) NA

Location of threat Hallway outside room 213

Intended victim or recipient of threat Rob Brown   Grade 7   (Male)/ Female

Who witnessed the threat? Mr. Williams (teacher) and two other students heard John threaten Rob.

What was the threat statement or behavior? John Smith threatened Rob with the statement, "I'm gonna blow your head off." Another student reported that John had told several students that he was "sick and tired of taking crap from Rob" and had talked about shooting him at the bus stop.

Where and when did the threat statement or behavior take place? Room 213 at 11:30 a.m. on 11/20.

Threat information: A student who wished to remain anonymous told Mr. Williams that John had told several students that he was "sick and tired of taking crap from Rob" and had talked about shooting him at the bus stop. According to this student, John complained that Rob often called him names and made fun of him at the bus stop. When Dr. Thomas interviewed John, John admitted that he had a gun at home but said he wouldn't use it. He denied telling other students that he was going to shoot Rob. He said Rob often teased him but that no one had done anything about it, so he had decided to fight back. He stated that Rob had pushed him as he walked out of science class. Rob denied pushing John and said he had no idea why John started a fight. He said he did not take John's threat seriously.

Threat response: John and Rob were suspended from school for ten days for fighting. John's threat was regarded as a substantive threat requiring police notification because it involved the mention of a firearm, there was a history of conflict between the two boys, and John had expressed an intention to harm Rob on other occasions. Based on the school division's Guidelines for Responding to Student Threats of Violence, the following actions were taken on 11/20: (1) Dr. Thomas notified school resource officer James Johnson; (2) Dr. Thomas met with John's mother when she arrived to pick him up. John's mother confirmed that John had a hunting rifle at home. She agreed to remove the weapon from his room and have a relative keep it until the situation was resolved. She agreed that John could participate in a mental health assessment with the school psychologist, Ms. Bronson; (3) Dr. Thomas met with Rob and his foster parents, Mr. and Mrs. Anderson, and informed them of John's threat. The Andersons agreed to instruct Rob not to go near John or interact with him; (4) A mental health assessment was completed with John on 11/24.

Action plan: The threat assessment team, consisting of Dr. Thomas, Ms. Bronson, Mr. Jones, and Officer Johnson, established a plan to maintain school safety and respond to John's educational needs. Officer Johnson met with John to review the potential legal ramifications of his actions on 11/21. Officer Johnson decided not to seek a court petition at this time but to monitor the situation for any further problems. John was referred to the school counselor to discuss the appropriateness of his behavior and to see whether he would be willing to attend a conflict mediation session with Rob. John saw the school counselor on 11/24 and participated in a conflict mediation session with Rob on 11/25. John will continue to see the counselor as needed. John's parents met with the principal on 11/26 and agreed to transport John to school by car until January and then to review the situation. School intervention with Rob is not included in this report. Both Officer Johnson and Mr. Jones will have contact with John at least weekly for the next three months. John has agreed to contact one of them if he is involved in conflict with any student. The principal will review this plan in 60 days or if there is any indication of further problems.

Principal's signature   Date

CHAPTER 5

MENTAL HEALTH ASSESSMENT OF THREATENING STUDENTS

WHAT IS THE PURPOSE OF THE MENTAL HEALTH ASSESSMENT?

The purpose of the mental health assessment is to maintain the safety and well-being of the student and potential victims. Therefore, the assessment has two objectives:

1. *Treatment and referral needs.* Assess the student's present mental state and determine whether there are urgent mental health needs that require attention, such as rage, psychosis, or risk of suicide. Beyond these immediate needs, consider whether there are other treatment, referral, or support needs.

2. *Threat reduction.* Gather information on the student's motives and intentions in making the threat. The goal of this component of the assessment is to understand why the threat was made and identify relevant strategies or interventions that have the potential to reduce the risk of violence.

The term "mental health assessment" is used to describe activities that fall within the scope of practice for school psychologists and other mental health professionals who work with students to assess psychological factors that affect their educational needs and ability to function at school. Team members always must consider local laws and regulations that guide their professional practice.

WHEN DO YOU CONDUCT A MENTAL HEALTH ASSESSMENT?

A mental health assessment should be conducted when a student makes a very serious substantive threat of violence. Because of the serious risk of violence, the assessment should begin as soon as possible after the threat is reported to authorities. The mental health professional may begin the assessment *without* parent permission in response to the immediate need to determine the safety of the student or others but should notify the student's parent or guardian promptly and obtain parent permission for further assessment. This assessment is similar to an assessment conducted when a student is suicidal because it must be conducted immediately for safety purposes.

As noted in Chapter 4, there are circumstances in which it may not be possible to conduct a complete mental health assessment, because the student either has been arrested or is not coming back to school. In some cases, a mental health assessment may be supplemented or shortened by the availability of other sources of information, such as a recent evaluation for special education services. Even with ample information from other sources, however, it is important to assess the student's current mental state and the circumstances surrounding the threat. It is unlikely that prior assessments, or assessments conducted by others, will have addressed the specific issues and concerns raised by the student's threat.

WHO DOES THE ASSESSMENT?

The assessment should be completed by a school staff member who is a mental health professional experienced in interviewing students and parents and familiar with concepts of threat assessment. In the two school divisions where these guidelines were field tested, the mental health assessments were conducted by school and clinical psychologists employed in the schools. In other school divisions, this assessment might be conducted by a social worker, counselor, or other mental health professional who has appropriate training and experience. In the absence of an available staff member, the school could contract with a community-based mental health professional who is trained and prepared to conduct the assessment following these guidelines; however, school-based professionals will be more knowledgeable of the school environment and experienced in working as a member of the school's threat assessment team.

HOW DOES THIS ASSESSMENT DIFFER FROM A VIOLENCE RISK ASSESSMENT?

The term "violence risk assessment" encompasses a broad category of assessments and could be construed to include the mental health assessment described here. However, there are some features of the mental health assessment that distinguish it from the usual violence risk assessment. Most importantly, this mental health assessment is *not intended to render a prediction whether the student will or will not commit a violent act.* The prediction of violence is a complex and difficult task, and communications about violence risk are easily misstated or misinterpreted (Borum, 1996). Although clinicians can make reasonably accurate short-term predictions of violence in some situations (Borum, 1996), little is known about the prediction of student violence, particularly in the context of active school intervention aimed at preventing violence (Mulvey & Cauffman, 2001). The mental health assessment is intended to gain understanding of the reasons for the student's

threat, so that a plan can be formulated by the team to address the problems or concerns that underlie the threat. This objective can be understood as a *risk reduction* or *risk management* approach, as distinguished from a purely predictive approach (Heilbrun, 1997).

Some school psychologists are reluctant to undertake a mental health assessment because they regard it as a violence risk assessment and are leery of making violence predictions. On the contrary, the assessment model described here is consistent with the school psychologist's role and professional expectations. School psychologists who are experienced in screening students for suicide potential will find that the mental health assessment requires similar interviewing skills and addresses similar issues. Moreover, the mental health assessment of a student who has threatened violence is consistent with the school psychologist's role in planning violence prevention programs (Furlong, Morrison, & Pavelski, 2000; Furlong, Paige, & Osher, 2003) and more generally in conducting a functional behavioral assessment and developing behavior intervention plans to address problems in a student's relationships with others (Drasgow & Yell, 2001). We believe that the two objectives of the mental health assessment—identification of immediate treatment needs and gathering information to develop a threat reduction plan— are consistent with school psychology training and practice, and so they capitalize on the school psychologist's strengths and expertise (Cole, 2003; Furlong et al., 2000).

IS THE ASSESSMENT CONFIDENTIAL?

In any assessment where violence is an issue, safety takes priority over confidentiality. No mental health professional can promise absolute confidentiality to a student (or anyone else), because the professional is obligated to seek help and protect potential victims if there is a clear and imminent danger to others (Borum, 1996). Team members should consult their state laws and practice regulations for guidance. Furthermore, the interviewer should explain to the student that he or she is working as part of a team and will share information with team members. It is helpful to emphasize to a student that this is his or her opportunity to tell his or her side of the story—to explain what happened and why from his or her perspective.

WHAT ARE THE SOURCES OF INFORMATION FOR THE MENTAL HEALTH ASSESSMENT?

The mental health professional should gather information from multiple sources and strive to obtain corroboration for key points or any facts that are in dispute. At a minimum, the mental health professional should interview the student and the student's parents or guardians. It would also be desirable to interview the intended victim or witnesses to the threat. Other sources of information should be used as appropriate to the circumstances of the threat, and, in some cases, it will be preferable to rely on information obtained by other team members.

POTENTIAL SOURCES OF INFORMATION

1. Student who made the threat (interview and optional testing)

2. Intended victim (may use principal's interview)

3. Witnesses to the threat (may use principal's interview)

4. Parent

5. Teacher or school staff member who knows the student best

6. School resource officer

7. Any professional providing mental health treatment or relevant court services worker (with parent permission)

8. School file (discipline record, grades, and previous evaluations or referrals)

DIRECTIONS FOR THE MENTAL HEALTH ASSESSMENT

The mental health assessment is designed to document the circumstances of a threat and the history and context of a student's behavior from multiple perspectives. It will include information about the student's school and family history as well as special circumstances that might shed light on the student's threat. It is not intended to justify the student's behavior but rather to explain the reasons why it occurred.

The questions listed in the following sections can be modified as appropriate to the situation and the student's age. Interviewers may alter the order of the questions and add questions as they deem appropriate, but they should not neglect the content areas defined by the questions. The interviewers should make use of all available sources of information, including previous psychological assessments, special education evaluations, and records from community agencies. However, the availability of information from previous assessments does not eliminate the need to interview the student about the threat and to cover risk factors for violence that would not have been considered in assessments conducted for other purposes.

The information obtained in this assessment should be summarized in a written report for the threat assessment team and can be placed in the confidential section of the student's file. This report is part of the school's safety evaluation. There may be a separate written safety report prepared by the threat assessment team that integrates the findings and recommendations from the mental health assessment.

OUTLINE FOR STUDENT INTERVIEW

Approach the student in a manner that seems appropriate to establishing rapport. It is often useful to include the question, "Do you know why I wanted to meet with you today?" After learning about the student's understanding of the meeting, spend some time explaining that the purpose of the interview is to understand why the threat incident took place and what should be done to ensure that the problem is resolved and no one is harmed. The student should understand that information from the interview will be shared with the school principal or other school staff in deciding what to do about the threat incident. Help the student understand that this is his or her opportunity to express concerns, describe the incident from his or her perspective, and generally have a voice in what will be decided.

Review of threat

1. What happened? What exactly did you say? What did you mean by that?

2. I know you must have had reasons to say that; can you explain what led up to it?

3. How would you do it (carry out the threat)?

4. What could happen that would make you want to do it (carry out the threat)?

5. What would happen if you did do it? (Review both the effects on intended victims and consequences for the student.)

6. What do you think the school should do in a situation in which a student makes a threat like this?

7. What were you feeling then? How do you feel now?

8. How do you think [the person threatened] felt?

Relationship with intended victim(s); ask about the specific intended victim(s)

1. How long have you known this person?

2. What has happened in the past between you and this person?

3. What do you think this person deserves?

4. Do you see any way that things could be improved between you and this person?

Stress

1. What kinds of things have been going on with you lately? What sorts of things have you worried about?

2. How has your schoolwork been going lately? Are there things you have been worried about with your schoolwork? Other things at school?

3. What is the worst thing that has happened to you lately? Have any other bad things happened? Is there something you regret or wish you could change?

4. Have there been any changes in your family? Has anyone been sick, moved away, or had anything bad happen to him or her?

5. Do you have any family members in jail or prison?

6. Do you take any medications?

7. Have you been involved in any counseling?

Family support

1. Whom do you live with in your family? Are there other family members you don't live with? Have there been any changes in the past year?

2. Whom in your family are you close to?

3. How well do your parents or guardians know you?

4. Where do you go after school? Where are your parents at this time? How much do your parents keep track of where you are or what you are doing?

5. How strict are your parents? What do they do to punish you? When was the last time you got in trouble with them? What was the worst time?

6. How did your parents react (or how will they react) when they found out about this situation?

Depression

1. What has your mood been like the past few weeks? Have you felt down or depressed at times? How bad has it been? (Be alert for statements of pessimism and hopelessness that might indicate suicide risk.)

2. Have you felt nervous or anxious? Irritable or short tempered? How bad has it been?

3. Have you ever felt like life wasn't worth living? Like maybe you would kill yourself?

4. Have you ever done something to hurt yourself on purpose? Ever cut yourself on purpose?

5. Have you had any problems with your sleep? Appetite? Energy level? Concentration?

6. Have you been taking any medications to help with your mood or for any other reason?

Note that, if there are indications of suicidal thoughts or feelings, there should be a more extensive assessment of suicide risk. If necessary, develop a plan for protecting the student and making appropriate referrals.

Psychotic symptoms

Ask a few probing questions and follow up if there is any indication of delusions or hallucinations. Phrase questions appropriate to the student's age and understanding.

1. Have you had any unusual experiences lately, such as hearing things that others cannot hear or seeing things that others cannot see?

2. Have you felt like someone was out to get you or wanted to harm you? Have you had any other fears that seem strange or out of the ordinary?

3. Do you have any abilities or powers that others do not have, such as ESP or reading minds?

4. Have you felt numb or disconnected from the world or felt like you were somehow outside your body?

Weapons

Ask about any weapons mentioned in the threat. As an example, these questions concern a threat made to stab someone.

1. You said that you were going to stab [name of victim]. What were you going to stab him with?

2. Do you have a knife? What kind of a knife is it (or, how would you get a knife)?

3. Have you ever had to use a knife with someone? What happened?

4. What do you think would happen if you did use a knife with [name of victim]?

Access to firearms

Ask about firearms in all cases, even if no firearm was mentioned. If the threat involved a knife, bomb, or other weapon, ask about that weapon too.

1. Do you have a gun?

2. Are there guns in your home? Have you ever used a gun for hunting or target shooting?

3. If you wanted a gun, how would you get one?

4. What do you think you might do if you had a gun?

5. Have you ever had to use a gun with someone? Have you ever thought about using a gun with someone?

Bullying

Bullying is broadly defined and may include teasing, social exclusion, or other forms of humiliation in addition to physical threats of violence. The student may not use the term "bully" and may be reluctant to admit being the victim of bullying behavior, so be prepared to rephrase questions and probe for victim experiences.

1. Is there anyone who has threatened you recently? Is there anyone who makes you feel afraid? (Ask about sexual threats if appropriate to the situation.)

2. Is there anyone who has teased you or picked on you recently? Is there anyone who has beat you up or pushed you around? How about at home?

In response to any positive answer, follow up for more information: How often does it happen? What have you tried to do about it? Did you let any adult know about this, and, if so, what happened? Be alert to statements indicating that a bullied student feels like there is no solution to the problem or is contemplating revenge.

43

Aggressive behavior

1. Do people treat you fairly? Who has been unfair with you lately? When people treat you unfairly, what do you do about it?

2. When you get angry, what do you do? Has your temper ever gotten you into trouble?

3. Do you get into fights? When was the last time? What happened?

4. Have you ever threatened to harm anyone before?

5. Have you thought about what it would be like to hurt someone really badly? Have you written any stories or made any drawings that are violent?

6. Have you ever set fire to things?

7. Have you damaged your own property or someone else's property?

8. Have you ever intentionally hurt an animal?

School discipline

1. When was the last time you got into trouble in school? What happened?

2. Have you ever been suspended or expelled?

3. Have your parents ever been called to school because of your behavior?

4. Do you ever cut school or certain classes?

5. Do you feel that the rules at this school are fair? What has been unfair?

Delinquent behavior

1. Have you been in trouble with the law or with police before? What happened?

2. Have you ever gone to juvenile court? What was it about?

3. Have you done things that could have gotten you arrested or in trouble with the law? What was the worst thing? What else?

4. Do you drink beer, wine, or other alcohol? Have you ever? How often do you drink? When was the last time? Tell me about it.

5. Do you smoke marijuana? Have you ever? How often? When was the last time?

6. Have you used any other drugs? How often? When was the last time? Tell me about it.

Exposure to violence

1. Do you see or hear of violence in your neighborhood?

2. Do you know anyone who was shot, stabbed, or beaten up really badly?

3. Do people argue much at home? Does anyone get physically aggressive?

4. What kind of movies do you like? What kind of video games do you enjoy playing? What are your favorite Internet sites?

Also ask the student about his or her reactions to any recent acts of violence in the news.

Peer relations

1. What are your friends like? Have you had any trouble with your friends lately? Who is your best friend?

2. How would your friends describe you?

3. Do you have a boyfriend or girlfriend? (Keep in mind that the student might not be heterosexual, and there may be concerns in this area.) How are things going with him or her? Did you have one before? What happened in that relationship?

4. Do you have friends who get in trouble?

5. Have you ever joined a gang or been part of a group like a crew, clique, posse, or mob?

6. Do any of your friends know about [refer to threat situation]? What was said about it? Is there anyone who feels the same way you do?

Coping

1. How do you like to spend your free time?

2. What kinds of things do you do well?

3. What are your hobbies and interests? What do you enjoy doing?

4. Can you think of a problem you faced in the past that worked out okay? Can you think of a problem that you solved? Can you think of a time when you went to someone about a problem and that person was able to solve it?

5. What are your plans for the future? What would you like to do when you finish school?

6. What could we do that would help with [refer to the problem that led to the threat]?

STUDENT TESTING

The mental health assessment may include the use of psychological testing to supplement the student interview. Testing may provide information about a specific issue in the assessment, such as quantifying the degree of depression, anxiety, or anger that a student is experiencing. In most schools, parent permission is required for psychological testing.

PARENT INTERVIEW

Understandably, parents may feel apprehensive, guilty, or defensive when being interviewed about their child's behavior. It is important that the interviewer find ways to convey respect for the parent, from initial contact to the interview's conclusion. Also, it should be evident that the interviewer is interested in understanding and helping the child; otherwise, the parent may regard the interview as an investigation designed to uncover evidence of wrongdoing by the student or incompetence by the parent. Overall, the interviewer should make every effort to engage the parent as an ally.

Parent knowledge of the threat

1. What do you (the parent) know about the threat?

2. Have you heard your child (or use child's name) talk about things like this before?

3. Are you familiar with [the intended victim]? (Ask about the child's history with the intended victim—previous relationship and interactions.)

4. Does your child have the means to carry out the threat (such as access to firearms)?

5. What are you planning to do about the threat? (Is the parent willing to work with the school to develop a plan to ensure that the threat will not be carried out and that the student's needs are addressed?)

School adjustment

1. Has your child ever been suspended or expelled from school?

2. Have you ever met with the school (e.g., teacher, counselor, principal) about concerns in the past? What happened, what was going on, and what was the outcome?

3. Has your child ever needed special help in school? Ever been retained?

4. Has your child ever been tested in school?

5. How does your child like school?

6. How often does your child do homework?

7. What are your child's teachers like?

Family relationships and current stressors

1. Who lives in the home?

2. Are there any important events that have affected your family or child? Ask about any recent or pending changes, such as:

   - Relocation of household, divorce or separation, death in the family, or other personal loss

   - Changes in financial or parents' employment status

   - Involvement of others in the home with the courts or the law

3. Whom does your child share concerns with? Whom is he or she close to?

4. How well does he or she get along with you? Siblings? What are the types of conflict, what are they about, and how are they resolved?

5. How does your child show anger toward you and other family members?

6. What does your child do after school? Who supervises him or her? What time is your child supposed to be home at night?

7. What responsibilities does your child have at home?

8. Does your child follow rules? What are the consequences for not following the rules?

Peer relations and bullying

1. Has your child reported being teased, intimidated, rejected, or bullied in some other way? If so, what have you done in response?

2. Who are your child's friends? Are you pleased or displeased with your child's choice of friends?

3. How much is your child influenced by peers? Are there any examples of your child doing something to please peers that caused him or her to be in trouble?

Delinquent behavior

1. Has your child been in trouble with the law or with police before? What happened?

2. Has your child ever gone to juvenile court? What was it about?

3. Has your child done things that could have gotten him or her arrested or in trouble with the law? What was the worst thing? What else?

4. Does your child drink beer, wine, or other alcohol?

5. Does your child smoke marijuana?

6. Has your child used any other drugs?

History of aggression

1. How does your child handle frustration?

2. When your child gets angry, what does he or she do?

3. Has your child ever been involved in a fight? When, where, and with whom?

4. Has your child's temper ever gotten him or her into trouble?

5. Has your child ever hit you or other family members?

6. Has your child destroyed his or her own things or someone else's property?

7. Does your child have any pets? Has he or she ever intentionally hurt the pet or some other animal?

Access to weapons

1. Do you have a gun in your home? Does your child have access to firearms through friends, relatives, or some other source?

2. Does your child have access to weapons other than firearms, such as military knives, martial arts weapons, or some other kind of weapon?

3. Has your child ever talked about using a weapon to hurt someone? Ever been in trouble for using a weapon, carrying a weapon, or threatening someone with a weapon?

4. What can you do to restrict your child's access to weapons?

Exposure to violence

1. Has your child ever been a victim of abuse?

2. Is your child exposed to violence in the neighborhood?

3. Do people argue much at home? Has there been any physical aggression at home?

4. What kinds of movies, video games, and Internet sites does your child like? Any restrictions? How is your child supervised? What is your child's response?

History

1. How old was your child when he or she started to walk? To talk? (Ask about any delays in cognitive, motor, or language development.)

2. Has your child ever had a problem with bedwetting? When and for how long? Was anything done for this?

3. Has your child ever been hospitalized? Had any serious illnesses?

4. Has your child had any recent medical treatment? Is he or she taking any medications? (Obtain diagnoses and medications. Ask for a release.)

Mental health

1. Does your child have problems paying attention? Does your child follow directions without repetition and reminders? Does your child complete activities on his or her own? Does your child say things without thinking? Is your child surprised by the consequences of his or her actions?

2. What has your child's mood been like the past few weeks?

3. Has your child been unusually nervous or anxious? Irritable or short tempered? How bad has it been?

4. Has your child had problems with sleep? Appetite? Energy level? Concentration?

5. Has your child ever talked about hurting himself or herself? Have you ever been concerned that he or she might be suicidal?

6. Have there been any times when your child seemed to be hearing things that weren't there? Has he or she said things that didn't make sense or seemed to believe in things that weren't real?

7. Has your child ever seen a counselor or therapist? Ever taken medication for his or her behavior or mood?

8. Has your child had any involvement with other agencies or programs in the community?

Behavior rating scales or checklists may be helpful in some cases to supplement the parent interview.

Willingness to assist in action plan

Explore with the parents how willing they are to support recommendations for treatment, school placement, and other possible interventions. Will the parents encourage the student to apologize or make amends with the person who was threatened? The parents' level of cooperativeness is a legitimate factor to consider in determining the safety of the student and whether it is feasible and safe for the student to return to school.

A frequent issue is that the victim of a threat, or the parents of a student who has been threatened, will want information about the student who made the threat and how the school is handling the situation. The desire for information is a legitimate safety concern, and sharing a limited amount of information can be helpful in lessening anxiety and restoring calm. Continued conflict between the parties can increase the risk of violence, so actions that reduce conflict and promote understanding can be useful. For these reasons, it is desirable to determine if the parent is willing to sign a release so that the team can share a limited amount of information with the person who was threatened (and, if the person is a minor, with the parents of the minor). This information might be limited to basic facts about the handling of the case (e.g., the student received a mental health assessment, was interviewed by the police, and has agreed to attend counseling sessions) without disclosing more personal information. If the student is possibly going to return to school, it would be a good idea to obtain permission from his or her parents to advise the victim of the threat when the student will be returning to school and under what conditions this will take place.

TEACHER OR STAFF INTERVIEW

Start by interviewing the school staff member who knows the student best. This may be a teacher, the school counselor, or any other school staff member. Interview any other staff members who have relevant information. For example, there may be a teacher from the previous year who knows more about the history of one student's conflict with another student.

The teacher or staff interview must be adapted to the individual situation and need not follow a structured format. It might be helpful to cover these topics:

Academics

1. How is this student doing academically? Has there been any change in recent weeks?

2. What are this student's verbal skills? How well can he or she express himself or herself in words?

3. Has this student been considered for special education or placed in special education? What kinds of difficulties does the student have? (If a student is receiving special education services, ask about any problem behaviors that are regarded as part of his or her disability. See a discussion of special education issues in Chapters 7 and 10.)

Teacher knowledge of the threat

1. What do you know about the threat?
2. Have you heard this student talk about things like this before?
3. What have other students told you about this incident?
4. Is there another teacher or staff member who might know something about this?

Student's peer relations

1. How well does this student get along with other students?
2. Who are the student's friends?
3. Are there students who do not get along with this student?
4. Have there been other conflicts or difficulties with peers?
5. Has this student ever complained of being bullied, teased, or treated unfairly by others?

Depression

1. Have there been any apparent changes in the student's mood, demeanor, or activity level? Has the student seemed withdrawn or apathetic?
2. Has the student expressed any attitudes that could imply depression, such as expressions of hopelessness or futility, inadequacy or shame, and self-criticism or worthlessness?
3. Has this student shown an increase in irritability or seemed short tempered?

Discipline

1. What kinds of discipline problems have you experienced with this student?

2. How does this student respond to being corrected by an adult?
3. What are the student's emotional responses to being disciplined?

Aggression

1. How does this student express anger?
2. Does this student seem to hold a grudge? Seem resentful?
3. Has this student done anything that expresses anger or aggression, or has the student expressed an aggressive theme in written assignments, drawings, class projects, and so on?

Parents

1. Have you had any contact with this student's parents? What happened?

MENTAL HEALTH ASSESSMENT REPORT

The Mental Health Assessment Report form contains the following sections.

Identifying information. Give the student's name, gender, age, grade, school, and other relevant identifying information.

Reason for referral. State that this assessment was requested by the school principal because the student made a threat of violence that was judged to be a very serious substantive threat. Describe the threat, including the exact statement or threatening behavior, and where and when it took place.

Sources of information. Describe or list the sources of information used in this report, including information from the principal, interviews with the student and witnesses, any parent interviews, and any psychological tests or scales administered.

Findings. Describe how the student presented and any important aspects of his or her mental state, including any indications or markers of mental disorder requiring further assessment or referral. Identify any stresses, conflicts, or unmet needs that affect the student's functioning or bear on the threat incident.

Review the student's understanding of the threat and its meaning from his or her perspective. Note whether the student has a history of violent or aggressive behavior, as well as any findings from the assessment that raise concerns about the student's potential for violence, such as access to firearms, gang membership, peer encouragement to fight, drug use, or inadequate home supervision.

Conclusions. In general, the mental health professional should not be expected to make a definitive statement that a student is or is not dangerous; such statements go beyond current knowledge in the field of risk assessment. The report may identify risk factors and protective factors, and it may express concerns where there appear to be compelling risk factors.

The report should present recommendations aimed at reducing the risk of violence, and these recommendations should convey the nature and degree of concern about the potential for violence. In all cases, the goal is to reduce the risk of violence rather than to predict violence. Recommendations may include a wide range of strategies but should address both any immediate safety needs to protect potential victims and broader efforts to resolve conflicts or problems that precipitated the threat.

There are two basic types of recommendations. First are recommendations for school behavior support, which are actions to be taken at school. The report should identify any signs of disability that would indicate the need for further assessment, child study, or special education evaluation. Procedures for implementing behavior plans are described in Chapter 10. Second, if appropriate, the report may propose other recommendations for the parents to consider implementing outside of school, such as seeking community-based services for the child.

A case example of a Mental Health Assessment Report is presented on the following pages.

Mental Health Assessment Report   CONFIDENTIAL

Name	John Dunn	**School**	Jefferson Middle School
Date of Birth	01/01/88	**Grade**	8
Date of Report	10/25	**Age**	13
Examiner	Ms. Franklin	**Gender**	Male

Reason for Referral

John Dunn is a 13-year-old student in the eighth grade at Jefferson Middle School, referred for a mental health assessment because he made a threat of violence that was judged by the principal, Dr. Smith, to be a very serious substantive threat. The purpose of this evaluation was to evaluate John's emotional state and motivation in making the threat, identify risk and protective factors for violence, and make recommendations intended to reduce the risk of violence. This report is not intended to make disciplinary recommendations or special education determinations.

According to the principal's investigation, Janet Jones, a seventh grade student, reported to the guidance counselor, Alice Carson, that on September 30 John showed her what he called a "hit list" containing names of several students who were friends or boyfriends of Janet. Janet reported that John was angry at her for breaking off their relationship and stated that he would "get even with you and all your friends by blowing them away with a shotgun."

Sources of Information

Interviews with John Dunn on October 1 and 8

Interview with John's mother, Ms. Barbara Dunn, on October 8

Interview with Dr. Abraham Smith, school principal

Interview with Alice Carson, guidance counselor

Interview with Jim Stockton, homeroom teacher

Interview with Officer David Williams, school resource officer

Telephone interview with Tom Adams, Region 10 caseworker

Region 10 records

School records

Findings

John is currently in the regular education program at Jefferson Middle School. His teacher described him as an average student who does not have a history of discipline problems at school. According to Mrs. Dunn, John was teased about his small stature in elementary school and was retained in the second grade following a school transfer. John has a history of attendance problems associated with his refusal to come to school and has missed six days this term. In the sixth grade, John reported to the school counselor that he was being bullied by two classmates. John was transferred to a different classroom, and there were no further reports of bullying.

John has been treated for major depression by the community services center for the past two years, following an attempted suicide by overdose of his mother's medication. He has been prescribed an antidepressant but discontinued its use during the summer because he felt he did not need it. John and his mother have also received in-home therapy from Tom Adams of the community services center.

John's parents separated following repeated episodes of domestic violence witnessed by John and his younger sister. A significant stressor is that there is chronic conflict between Mrs. Dunn and her estranged husband, and John feels alienated from his father and fears there will be further physical altercations between his parents.

During two clinical interviews, John presented as cooperative but guarded and sometimes hesitant to answer questions. He communicated in a clear and coherent manner, and there was no indication of psychosis such as delusions or hallucinations. His mood appeared depressed, and he acknowledged having trouble sleeping at night and sometimes feeling like he was "not a good person, like nobody likes me." He denied both current and past suicidal thoughts but, when confronted about his overdose two years ago, admitted past thoughts of killing himself because he was angry with his parents.

John stated that he has been angry for several weeks because a classmate named Janet Jones had broken off their friendship and started teasing him. He believes that a male student, described as her "new boyfriend," is responsible for her teasing him. The male student is one of two boys reported to have bullied John in the sixth grade. John believes that this student and several other boys enjoy teasing him and have written insulting notes that they slipped into his locker. John stated that he prepared a list of the boys' names and showed it to Janet in order to frighten them. He denied any intention to shoot them or physically harm them in any way, stating, "I just wanted to make them stop what they were doing. They were messing with me and I was messing back."

By all accounts, John does not have a history of fighting or other violent behavior. He denies violent fantasies but admits to being angry with his classmates. He denied having access to a firearm. Officer David Williams reported that he visited the Dunn residence as part of his investigation of the incident. Mrs. Dunn assured Officer Williams that there were no firearms in the home and permitted him to search the residence. Officer Williams met with John and explained to him the potential seriousness of the situation. John has consistently expressed regret for his behavior to school authorities and to Officer Williams. In his interview for this evaluation, John expressed a willingness to resolve the conflicts with his classmates.

Conclusions

This evaluation identified both risk and protective factors for violence. The primary risk for violence is that John is embroiled in an ongoing conflict with other students. He feels bullied and teased by several classmates and rejected by a former girlfriend. He is angry with these students, perceives that adults have not been able to protect him from mistreatment, and wants to retaliate. He is also experiencing the stress of a difficult family situation and has witnessed violence at home. He has been treated for major depression but has discontinued his medication despite current symptoms of depression.

There are several protective factors. John realizes his threatening behavior was inappropriate and wrong, and he is willing to engage in a process to resolve the conflict. He does not have a history of violent behavior. Although his family is under stress, his mother is cooperative and supportive of school efforts to address John's threat. There are treatment resources available to John and his mother, including an in-home therapist and psychiatric consultation, although they have not yet been brought to bear on John's problems with his peers.

This evaluation generated the following recommendations, which could be implemented through a school behavior support plan:

1. There should be immediate efforts to resolve the conflict between John and his peers. As previously discussed with the guidance department, Ms. Carson should interview the other students and obtain their side of the story.

2. In separate meetings, John and the other students involved in this conflict should receive instruction on school policy concerning bullying. John should be required to report all incidents of bullying or harassment to a specific staff member at school. The students alleged to have bullied John should be advised about the consequences of this behavior and should be disciplined for any bullying that can be confirmed. It may be appropriate for the school resource officer to meet with some of the students involved in the alleged bullying.

3. When John is permitted to return to school, his class schedule should be modified to reduce his contact with the other students named on his list. The guidance department confirms that such a schedule change is a viable option. His locker should be moved to a new location away from these students. Each of the students involved in the conflict should be told to refrain from interaction with John, and John should be told the same with respect to the other students.

4. John should continue to participate in in-home family therapy with Tom Adams. Because of the risk factors noted above, it would be advisable for John to participate in individual therapy that addresses his depression, anger, peer relations, and understanding of the consequences of aggressive behavior.

5. John should be required to meet with the school resource officer to review the consequences of making threats against others and to establish an understanding that the officer is at the school to help ensure his safety as well as that of other students.

6. The school guidance counselor should meet with John and schedule a series of appointments for the purpose of monitoring his state of mind and his peer relations. There should be a plan for John to contact the school counselor or another school staff member anytime there is an incident or problem with his peers.

7. John's mother should agree to ask the school counselor to keep her informed with regard to how John is doing and to notify her immediately if there are further problems with John's peers. Another recommendation for John's parents to consider is that John return for psychiatric consultation to determine the appropriateness of resuming antidepressant medication.

These recommendations are intended for consideration by the principal and other school staff in developing a safety plan for John. This report and the safety plan should be placed in the confidential section of John's student file and made available for parent review.

CHAPTER 6

PATHWAYS TO YOUTH VIOLENCE

WHAT FACTORS INDICATE A STUDENT IS VIOLENT?

Threat assessment would be much easier if there were a single set of factors or a profile that indicated whether a student was violent. Unfortunately, violence is not the product of any single set of factors, and there is no magic number of factors that crosses the threshold into violence. There are multiple constellations or patterns of factors that can generate violent behavior. For this reason, checklists of warning signs have limited value. The pattern of factors is more important than the number of factors. A malignant combination of two or three factors may be more dangerous than a lengthy list of factors that do not cohere around a motive and plan for violence. Research on juvenile homicide offenders has identified three common patterns of youth violence (Benedek & Cornell, 1989; Cornell, 1990; Cornell, Benedek, & Benedek, 1987; Cornell, 1999). Knowledge of these patterns can be useful in organizing the findings from the mental health assessment and safety evaluation.

1. Antisocial pathway

Youth traveling an antisocial pathway, which is the most common pathway, have a history of early childhood behavior problems and academic difficulties that are usually evident in the primary grades. There may be problems getting along with peers, refusal to accept adult authority, and general rule breaking. Sometimes these youth are diagnosed with learning disabilities or attention deficit disorder, but such conditions do not really account for the full range of the youth's behavior problems. In adolescence, there are escalating problems with delinquency, including fights, drug or alcohol use, and stealing. There may be gang involvement or an association with other delinquent peers who encourage violence. Typical acts of violence are directed at members of rival groups, peers who offend them, or authority figures who punish them. They also may commit acts of violence in the course of a robbery, burglary, rape, or some other crime.

These youth often have poor social skills and limited problem-solving abilities. They resort to violence because it is one of the few coping mechanisms they have in their repertoire, and in fact they may have found it to be successful in a variety of situations. These youth have overly positive attitudes toward the use of force and regard aggressive behavior as an effective means of reaching goals and attaining status among peers. Such youth often have verbal intellectual deficits and lack the expressive language skills that would be required for nonviolent methods of solving problems.

The most serious subgroup of antisocial youth have psychopathic traits. Psychopathy has been defined best through the Psychopathy Checklist: Youth Version (PCL:YV) (Forth, Kosson, & Hare, 2003). Some of the prominent characteristics of psychopathy are (1) superficial charm and an ability to engage others, often for manipulative purposes; (2) pervasive dishonesty and lying, with apparent enjoyment in deceiving others; (3) lack of empathy for others or remorse for one's actions, a seeming inability to experience feelings of guilt, and a tendency to rationalize harm to others and disown responsibility for one's actions; and (4) repetitive rule breaking and antisocial behavior in multiple forms. Psychopathy should be assessed by clinicians experienced with the PCL:YV, recognizing that the construct of psychopathy in adolescence is less well validated than in adult psychopathy, and, accordingly, the emphasis should be placed on psychopathic features rather than a formal psychopathy diagnosis (Murrie, Cornell, Kaplan, McConville, & Levy-Elkon, 2004).

2. Conflict pathway

Some youth reach a violent outcome because they become embroiled in an emotional conflict or dispute with someone. They may have few antisocial characteristics, and in some cases observers are stunned because the youth had no apparent proclivity toward criminal violence. Many are not problem students and may even be seen as good students. Some youth are especially vulnerable to conflicts that lead to violence because they are unusually sensitive to teasing, criticism, or rejection. They may be victims of bullying, but it is not necessary that the bullying be extremely cruel or beyond what some of their classmates might experience. Their heightened vulnerability to bullying makes its effect more severe.

These youth experience intense feelings of shame and humiliation, either in response to bullying or because of some disappointment in their lives. Disappointments can range from rejection in a dating relationship to failure to attain an academic goal. The result is that the youth becomes depressed and may be suicidal. Especially of concern is a youth's perception that the future is hopeless and that the only thing that matters is obtaining relief from distress. Often there is an accumulation of disappointments, stresses, or conflicts that may not be related to one another but that have a cumulative effect on the youth's judgment and perception of reality.

These youth may have long-standing feelings of resentment or feelings of being treated unjustly by others over a long period of time. These feelings culminate in explosive acts of revenge, often with the irrational belief that nothing else matters other than taking revenge or

taking action to repudiate criticism or rejection by others. Their victims may be classmates who mistreat them and, in some classic cases, parents who were chronically abusive and demanding. In some cases, the parents were not truly abusive but were perceived as excessively demanding and demeaning.

3. Psychotic pathway

The psychotic pathway, which is the least common pathway to violence, involves the development of serious mental disorders such as schizophrenia or bipolar disorder. Unless these students are having their first psychotic episode, it is likely that they have already been identified for special education services. It should be noted that the presence of mental illness alone does not mean the youth is violent, but in recent years studies have demonstrated that serious mental illness does indeed carry an increased risk of violence for some in this population (Silver & Teasdale, 2005).

Youth suffering from psychotic disorders that lead them to engage in violent acts typically have paranoid delusions that justify violence against someone. They may believe that someone is trying to harm them and they must defend themselves, or they may believe that someone is evil or dangerous and must be attacked. They may believe that someone is causing their chronic feelings of anxiety or distress, which are in fact products of the mental illness. They may believe that someone is ridiculing them, plotting against them, or doing something else that angers them and elicits an impulse to violence. Youth with psychotic disorders also may have auditory hallucinations—typically voices that criticize or demean them or prod them to act in a violent manner.

These youth also may have odd mannerisms or behaviors that elicit peer teasing and rejection. They may have an obsession with violence or with hostile feelings toward some individual or group of individuals. Older teens may have developed substance abuse problems as a way to self-medicate their anxiety and cope with their psychotic experiences.

WHAT FACTORS INCREASE THE RISK OF VIOLENCE?

Although no single factor or specific combination of factors will necessarily produce violent behavior, it is important to identify problem areas or circumstances that can increase the likelihood of violence. The FBI threat assessment report (O'Toole, 2000) recommends a four-pronged model. In each area, there are factors that—when present in an appropriate context—could indicate increased risk of violence. In many cases, these factors can become the target of interventions or recommendations to reduce risk. Here is a review of risk factors that are derived largely from the FBI report, organized into four domains (O'Toole, 2000). None of the traits by themselves indicate that violence will occur, and there are many individuals with some combination of these traits who are not violent. The team must consider the context for these factors and any specific evidence that the student is engaged in preparation to carry out the threat.

1. Personality traits and behaviors

Leakage of intentions. Leakage occurs when a person intentionally or unintentionally reveals thoughts or plans of committing a violent act. Leakage may take place for a variety of reasons, ranging from boastfulness and a desire to impress others to a preoccupation with violence that pervades everyday activities and conversation. There may be leakage because the person wants others to recognize that a problem exists and to intervene. An attempt by the student to recruit accomplices in a violent act or to warn persons whom he or she wants to protect from harm should be taken seriously.

Another form of leakage is repeated hints, indirect warnings, and indirect references to some impending event. There also may be drawings and writings that have an excessively violent theme. It may be difficult to distinguish this behavior from

idle fantasy or creativity, but investigate carefully if a youth appears frequently preoccupied with violent ideas. If the writings or drawings refer to specific individuals such as classmates or school staff, a threat assessment should be undertaken.

Aggressive traits. Youth who have a history of aggressive behavior are the most likely to engage in aggressive behavior. A youth with a history of fighting is likely to fight again, and a youth with a history of bullying others is likely to continue bullying. For this reason, it is essential to obtain a careful history and to corroborate the youth's report with information from other sources.

A theme in most of the preceding descriptions is a propensity toward excessive anger. Two different patterns may be present. Youth with *undercontrolled* anger are quick to flare up and express their anger repeatedly in aggressive behavior. They have frequent fights and generally seem to be hotheaded and volatile. In contrast, other youth exhibit *overcontrolled* anger. They have great difficulty expressing angry feelings and often control their anger even in situations where some expression of anger would be appropriate. Their anger simmers over time and eventually reaches a boiling point. They have infrequent episodes of anger that are unexpected and out of proportion to the circumstances. At other times they may appear excessively meek and inoffensive toward others.

Some youth will demonstrate a fascination with violence through movies, computer games, music, or other forms of entertainment. They may also have strong interests in guns, bombs, knives, warfare, or other topics associated with violence. They may have located Web sites that promote violence or antisocial attitudes. In response to violent news events, they may display identification with the aggressors rather than sympathy for victims.

Paranoid and schizotypal traits. Look for classic paranoid and schizotypal symptoms such as ideas of reference—the false belief that others are talking about them or that certain events are in reference to them. These youth have a heightened self-consciousness and a tendency to interpret even the most benign or irrelevant events as personally relevant. There also may be odd beliefs or magical thinking, ranging from superstitiousness to belief in special sensory powers (e.g., ESP). Such youth may be attracted to the occult or have bizarre interests and fantasies.

These youth are highly sensitive to teasing. Their obvious discomfort may invite more teasing and escalate the problem. Bullying has a catastrophic impact on their self-esteem and drives them to seek any means of relief or compensation. Such victims say things like, "Nothing else matters other than making them stop" or "I would do anything to get back at them."

Related to this problem, the youth may have a keen sense of being treated unfairly. Sometimes termed "injustice collectors," these youth have a long memory for unfair treatment and can recite a litany of mistreatment over a period of years. Over time, feelings of resentment over perceived injustice allow them to rationalize extreme acts of revenge.

The risk of violence is increased when a youth feels suspicious and mistrustful of others. This mistrust may border on outright paranoia or a false belief that others are exploiting or taking advantage of him or her. It may be especially difficult to establish good rapport because the youth fears that you, too, will be against him or her.

Most people are inhibited from violent behavior because they have empathy for others and find it painful to contemplate harming someone. This inhibition may be lessened or removed because the paranoid or schizotypal youth is emotionally detached from others. There may be a coldness and lack of feeling for the plight of others, even family members and friends.

Depressive traits. Many youth who commit unexpected acts of violence are seriously depressed. Their depression stems from disappointment in themselves and feelings of inadequacy or rejection, which may have been provoked by bullying, a failed relationship, or some other unhappy event. Depressed youth feel alienated from their peers, even if there is no basis for their feelings in how their friends treat them. They may provoke rejection by pulling away from friends or by lashing out at them in anger.

In a depressive state, they lose a rational perspective on their problems and see matters as more serious than others perceive them to be. This may progress to feelings of hopelessness and despair, leading to thoughts of suicide. Suicidal youth who have an identified enemy or antagonist may come to the desperate conclusion that there is nothing left to lose, so they might as well retaliate or take revenge.

Narcissistic traits. Narcissism refers to a combination of personality characteristics that involve self-centeredness, an intense need for attention and approval, a lack of concern for others, and an inflated self-image. Many of the other traits seen in aggressive individuals can be organized around a core of narcissism. Markers of narcissism include observations that the youth craves excitement, status, and power to a degree not observed in other adolescents; however, keep in mind that adolescence often invokes periods of narcissism as the adolescent struggles to develop a sense of identity. A youth with pathological narcissism exaggerates his or her accomplishments, constantly seeks recognition from others, and does not appear to have other resources for self-esteem and satisfaction. Narcissism is particularly difficult to assess when a youth has special talents or abilities that garner justifiable attention and praise.

Another indication of problematic narcissism is observed when the youth becomes enraged because his or her needs for status and approval are thwarted. Disappointment or failure that seems intolerably humiliating will trigger a violent reaction. Although the youth may outwardly appear confident, arrogant, and self-aggrandizing, this behavior has a defensive function, compensating for underlying feelings of inferiority and abandonment that may not be apparent except in rare breaks in defensiveness.

Psychopathic traits. Much less is known about psychopathy in adolescence than in adulthood, and there is reason to be cautious about employing a formal diagnosis of psychopathy in adolescence. Psychopathy has a pejorative connotation, and youth with psychopathic characteristics may not necessarily exhibit psychopathy as adults. However, studies have found that youth with psychopathic *characteristics* or who score highly on *juvenile psychopathy measures* have relatively high levels of conduct disorder and aggressive behavior (Murrie et al., 2004; Stafford & Cornell, 2003). Psychopathy is predictive of aggressive and assaultive behavior in psychiatric and correctional settings.

Psychopathy is associated with the narcissistic and aggressive traits described previously, as well as some additional features. The individual manifesting psychopathic qualities may be superficially charming, glib, and personable. He or she may be engaging and witty, exuding a confidence and air of superiority that less confident peers find attractive. These qualities make it possible for him or her to influence or manipulate others. Some leaders of youth gangs have compelling psychopathic characteristics.

These youth may be scornful of conventional values, rules, and laws. They are not inhibited by fear of punishment before they act, and afterward they do not feel guilty or remorseful for their actions. They tend to disown personal responsibility and to blame others. Even victims "get what they had coming" or "deserve it for being so stupid." They may be skillful, habitual liars. They may lie to evade responsibility, to impress you, or to obtain satisfaction from deceiving others.

A youth with psychopathic traits may engage in reckless behavior with little concern for the consequences. Many have a history of getting away repeatedly with criminal or outrageous acts, so that they become bolder and more daring over time. They are impulse ridden, thrill seeking, and attracted to dangerous activities.

2. Family dynamics

There is no single family pattern associated with youth violence. However, probably the most common pattern is the family with parents who have poor parenting skills and little commitment to parenting their children. The parents usually have an array of personal adjustment problems, such as substance abuse, domestic violence, marital instability, and irregular employment. They are too burdened by other demands to attend to their children. They lack motivation as well as skills to discipline their children. These families are most common in the cases involving students on an antisocial pathway.

A second, overlapping pattern is found in families who engage in harsh discipline on an irregular basis. These parents espouse interest in child rearing but are very inconsistent and often neglect to supervise their children. When a problem does come to their attention, they react in a highly punitive manner and may be physically or emotionally abusive to their children. They may be role models for bullying or the use of aggression to control and coerce others.

Finally, there are some parents who seem to be reasonably invested in caring for their children and who demonstrate adequate parent skills but who underestimate their child's needs for supervision and management. They may be distracted from child rearing by their own emotional needs or interpersonal stress (e.g., marital conflict or divorce, parental depression, employment problems), or they may be overly permissive for philosophical reasons. They may be too passive or indulgent of their child's wishes. Their approach may be adequate for most children but not if they have a child who is unusually impulsive or aggressive.

3. School dynamics

There is relatively little research on characteristics of schools that are associated with increased violent behavior; however, it is known that crime levels in a school are correlated with poverty and crime levels in the surrounding community. School crime is most often a reflection of community norms and practices. And interpersonal conflicts and disputes that arise in the community often continue in school.

School climate does have an effect on behavior problems at school. Research on school improvement suggests that schools can reduce behavior problems and discipline referrals by having clear, consistent discipline policies that are enforced in a fair, evenhanded manner. Student perception that discipline is lax or unfair may contribute to some forms of misbehavior.

Bullying is widely regarded as a problem that is easily affected by the attitudes of school staff. Many students believe that school authorities ignore bullying or refuse to intervene, and many victims of bullying fail to seek help (Unnever & Cornell, 2004). In schools where bullying is tolerated or overlooked, there may be more frequent victimization. Unless students have confidence and trust in school staff, they are unlikely to seek help or report threats of violence.

More controversial are suggestions that schools might encourage bullying and violence. Staff may model bullying behavior through their interactions with students. For example, staff who tease or belittle students as a form of discipline may encourage similar behavior by students. Some schools may institutionalize practices that promote bullying, for example, by permitting older students to haze younger students. Common forms of institutional bullying include so-called school traditions of initiating students into clubs, marching bands, or athletic teams. Sometimes school staff espouse philosophies that directly or indirectly encourage violent behavior. In one case, a football coach counseled students that the only way to resolve a conflict was to show that you were willing to fight and that a fight was inevitable in some situations.

4. Social dynamics

Some authorities contend that peers have more influence on adolescents than parents, and perhaps many parents would agree. From any perspective, association with deviant or antisocial peers can be a strong risk factor for violence. Adolescents will engage in risk-taking behavior or antisocial acts as part of a group that they would never consider if acting alone. Youth may be influenced by peers in a number of ways, ranging from direct pressure to participate in crime to the suspension of good judgment and inhibition when part of a crowd.

Younger adolescents may wish to impress older youths by engaging in high-risk activities, or they may be susceptible to manipulation by older peers who do not want to take the risk themselves. For example, two youths may convince a younger peer to carry a firearm or to commit a robbery while they stand as lookouts or drive the getaway vehicle.

Youth who belong to gangs have perhaps the highest risk of violent behavior. Studies show that gang members engage in more violent and other serious crimes than other youth. Moreover, youth who claim membership in a group they call a "gang" have higher levels of criminal activity than youth who claim membership in a "clique," "crew," or some other kind of group (Amato & Cornell, 2003).

Even if youth do not associate with violent peers, life in a high-crime neighborhood can foster aggressive attitudes and encourage violent behavior. Youth may become desensitized to violence, or they may feel that violence is an everyday part of life and a more or less inevitable experience. They may have increased access to handguns and may be encouraged to carry weapons to protect themselves. They may be more likely to find themselves in dangerous situations by chance.

Other social dynamics have to do with the level of acceptance a youth experiences in his or her neighborhood. Youths who are new to a neighborhood or who stand out because of their ethnic background or religion may be more vulnerable to bullying.

Copycat effects are another important social dynamic. Adolescents as well as adults are influenced by the actions of others. High-publicity crimes, suicides, and acts of violence can stimulate some individuals to commit similar acts. It is important to determine whether a youth has knowledge of recent events that might stimulate acts of violence. These events might be reported by the news media, or they may be events in the neighborhood. Youth also may be likely to imitate actions of immediate acquaintances or relatives. If a family member has spent time in prison or is a gang member, a youth may feel it is desirable, or even inevitable, to follow the same path.

CHAPTER 7

FREQUENTLY ASKED QUESTIONS

The questions in this chapter cover issues that are commonly raised by school staff during training workshops. Keep in mind that there are differences in state laws and regulations, as well as regional differences in school division policies, that could modify or qualify the answers to these questions. Also, new court decisions and new legislation make school policies and practices an evolving process. School authorities are advised to consult their local legal and governmental authorities for further guidance.

FAQ TOPICS

Bullying

Confidentiality

Gangs

Liability

Off-grounds threats

Parent notification

Record keeping

School resource officers

Searches

Special education

Types of threats

Zero tolerance

BULLYING

What is bullying? Many threats involve bullying, but bullying must be distinguished from ordinary peer conflict. Bullying takes place when one student subjects a student of lesser status or strength to repeated verbal abuse or threats of physical harm. A conflict between equals does not constitute bullying. So-called social or relational bullying occurs when one student causes another to be rejected, shunned, or excluded by peers. Bullying can involve more than one bully and more than one victim. Sometimes bullying comes to the attention of school authorities only when the victim makes a threat to retaliate against the bully. A victim might threaten to use a weapon or bring in the assistance of other students against the bully. These cases are complicated because there may be inappropriate behavior on both sides.

How should I handle a threat that involves bullying? In all cases, it is important to confront the bully and correct his or her behavior with instruction, counseling, and discipline. Victims of bullying are often reluctant to seek help because they are embarrassed or because they fear reprisals. School staff should emphasize the importance of seeking help for bullying and monitor the situation so that reprisals do not occur. Parents of bullies and victims should be involved throughout the process. Bullies must be sternly warned about the consequences of any further harassment or an attempt to retaliate against a victim. It is sometimes useful to bring bullies and victims together to resolve a dispute, but these meetings require skillful adult supervision so that the victim is not intimidated. Peer mediation is not appropriate for bullying because the two parties are not equal in status and the victim is at a disadvantage. See Chapter 9 for more information about schoolwide bullying prevention efforts.

CONFIDENTIALITY

Can I notify other school staff about a student threat of violence? Absolutely. According to the Family Educational Rights and Privacy Act (FERPA) (1974), disciplinary action taken against a student for conduct that poses a significant risk to the safety or well-being of that student or others can be disclosed to school staff who have legitimate interests in the behavior of that student (see § 99.36(b) 2). In some cases, it may be legitimate to notify all school staff, because all school staff members share responsibility for maintaining safety throughout the school.

Can I share information with the school resource officer about a student? Yes. School personnel are entitled to share information about students with school resource officers. This information should be relevant to the school resource officer's role in maintaining safety and security.

Can I notify staff at another school about a student threat of violence? Yes. FERPA (1974) says that disciplinary information and related information about a student's behavior can be disclosed to staff of another school who have legitimate educational interests in the behavior of that student (see § 99.36 (b) 3). It would be appropriate to notify staff of another school if the student who made the threat was transferring or advancing to that school. It would also be appropriate to notify staff of another school if your student had threatened a student at that school.

Can I notify parents about a student threat of violence? Yes. FERPA (1974) permits release of confidential information for safety reasons in a potentially dangerous situation. If a student has threatened to commit a violent act, it is important to notify the parents of the student, so that they can take appropriate protective action and supervise their child. It is also appropriate to notify the person who has been threatened and, if that person is a student, to notify the student's parents or guardians. See the section on parent notification later in this chapter.

GANGS

What if a threat involves gang members? Gang rivalries frequently lead to threats and acts of violence, and gang membership is a factor that increases a student's risk of violence. It follows that a threat made by gang members is more likely to be substantive than a threat by nonmembers. School personnel should report gang activity to local law enforcement and notify parents whose child is identified as a gang member. In some cases, gang disputes can be settled by professional mediation.

LIABILITY

If a student seriously injures another student, will the school be liable? In almost all cases, no. Courts have generally found that schools are not held responsible for student-on-student violence, even in the high-profile cases of school shootings. Nevertheless, from a liability perspective, schools generally should (1) have clear policies that meet prevailing standards for safety and security; (2) follow these policies in their practices; and (3) maintain adequate documentation of their decisions and actions in adherence to their policies. The definition of "prevailing standards" is subject to interpretation, but following your state's Department of Education guidelines and adopting practices supported by recognized educational authorities should be sufficient. The Threat Assessment Documentation form can be found in the Appendix.

Are there any circumstances under which the courts have found schools liable for damages resulting from student threats and related acts of violence? The U.S. Supreme Court ruled in *Davis v. Monroe County Board of Education* (1999) that a school board was liable under Title IX for student-on-student sexual harassment under the following conditions: (1) school authorities had knowledge of the harassment; (2) school authorities were deliberately indifferent to the harassment; and (3) the sexual harassment was so severe, pervasive, and objectively offensive that it deprived the victim of access to educational opportunities and benefits. In this case, a fifth grade girl was sexually harassed, verbally and physically, by a classmate on numerous occasions. The school administration took no corrective actions despite numerous incidents that were brought to its attention. Eventually, the family went to the police, and the boy was charged with sexual battery and pleaded guilty.

OFF-GROUNDS THREATS

What if a threat takes place off school property? If a threat takes place at a school-sponsored event or while the students are traveling to or from school, the incident should be handled like any other incident that takes place at school: Apply the existing school discipline policy and conduct a threat assessment.

If a threat occurs off school property and not during a school-related activity, the situation is more complex. Generally, schools cannot apply their disciplinary policies to students for transgressions that do not occur at school or during school events. (However, if a student commits a major crime, schools might decide to bar the student from returning to school for safety reasons.) Nevertheless, if a threat has been reported to school personnel, it is appropriate to conduct a threat assessment for safety purposes. If the threat is substantive, the team should determine what protective action is appropriate to maintain school safety.

PARENT NOTIFICATION

Can I notify parents that their child has been threatened at school without violating confidentiality? Yes. You *should* notify parents anytime their child has been threatened with an act of violence. Safety takes precedence over confidentiality. In fact, federal law (FERPA, 1974) says:

An educational agency or institution may disclose personally identifiable information from a school record to appropriate parties in connection with an emergency if knowledge

of the information is necessary to protect the health or safety of the student or other individuals. [§ 99.36 (a)]

In some cases, the fact that a student threatened a classmate may not be a part of the student's record, and, in these cases, there is no FERPA restriction on communication. FERPA applies only to information in a student's school records. You may want to consider your own school division's policy, but in general we recommend that school administrators have the option of contacting parents when their child has been threatened.

What do I tell the parents of a child who has been threatened? The decision to contact parents is up to the school administrator and depends on the circumstances, but in general it is best to contact parents. In many cases, a student will have participated in the resolution of the threat, perhaps by receiving an apology or attending a mediation session. In cases like these, it seems prudent to contact parents, explain what has taken place, and allay fears or concerns that might arise if you did not communicate with them.

Parent contacts for transient threats differ from parent contacts for substantive threats. In the case of a transient threat, you do not contact parents in order to warn them about a potential danger to their child, because transient threats are threats that have been resolved. You would contact the parents in order to advise them of how the threat was resolved, in anticipation that they might learn of the incident from their child. Also, the occurrence of a transient threat indicates that there might be conflict or a dispute between students, and, in this situation, it is reasonable and appropriate to notify the parents that this conflict or dispute exists.

In the case of a substantive threat, you have an obligation to warn parents that their child has been threatened. Tell the parents the basic facts about the threat (e.g., who said what to whom, where, and when). Parents should know the name of the student or students who made the threat. In addition, be sure to explain to parents the steps you took to keep their child safe, informing them that the school has standard procedures for evaluating a threat and taking steps to prevent a threat from being carried out. You also might want to inform parents that you have consulted with the school resource officer (or another law enforcement officer), a school counselor or psychologist, and the other student's parents, and that you are working with the student who made the threat.

Parents may well be alarmed that their child has been threatened, but a calm, factual approach may help reassure them and engage their support and cooperation. In some cases, parents may be worried that the school is not doing enough to ensure their child's safety. It is worthwhile to listen to the parents' concerns and consider their merit. School administrators should resist being pressured to take security precautions that are not considered necessary by the threat assessment team or by law enforcement. The school administrator may want to take the parents' requests under advisement until they can be considered by the threat assessment team. The parents' initial reactions may be stronger and more emotional than their responses when some time has passed and they have had an opportunity to speak with their child.

Anticipating a strong response, some administrators are reluctant to notify parents that their child has been threatened. However, failure to notify parents that their child has been threatened is likely to arouse greater concern than letting them know that you are on top of the situation and taking action.

I notified the parents that a student threatened their child. Some time has passed and now these parents want more information. What can I tell them? If there is any continuing threat to their child, parents should be informed. Safety takes priority over confidentiality. It also seems reasonable to let parents know—in general terms—what steps have been taken to ensure their child's safety. If the student who made the threat is returning to school, we recommend that the principal call the parents or, in some cases, meet with the parents of the threatened student, for the purpose of assuring

them that their child will remain safe in the school. Without going into details, the principal can explain that the student who is returning to school has done what was required, has been carefully evaluated, and is considered ready to return to school. Even if there is information you cannot provide to the parents, you can listen to their concerns, promise to monitor the situation closely, offer reassurance, and invite them to contact you again if they learn of anything that raises their concerns.

The threat assessment team should plan carefully for a student's return to school. As part of this plan, the team might request that the student and the student's parents give permission for you to notify the parents of the victim(s) of the threat. It also might be desirable to have the student give a written or oral apology to the victims and assure them that the matter has been settled. These steps might help ease the student's return to school and reassure the victims and their parents.

Everyone in the school knows about the threat a student made, and many parents are concerned. What can I tell them? When the learning environment has been disrupted by a student's threat, or rumors about a threat, school administrators are justified in taking reasonable steps to dispel rumors, quell fears, and restore order. In these cases, it is appropriate to send home a short letter to parents advising them of the threat and assuring them that the situation is under control. Unless the entire community is in danger, there is no need to reveal the student's name.

A general letter should provide enough information to dispel rumors and to assure parents that responsible action is being taken. A common example would be a false bomb threat. A false bomb threat is usually a transient threat (unless the student harbors a continuing intent to harm someone), but nevertheless it is a serious legal violation and can be very disturbing. It would be appropriate for a school principal to send out a letter to parents informing them that the threat took place and what was done about it.

Here are the points you should cover in a parent notification letter:

- Acknowledge that a threat was made and describe the nature of the threat. ("A student called in a bomb threat this morning at 8:30 a.m. We immediately evacuated the school as a safety precaution.")

- Assure parents that the school is following its policy on threats. ("The police were contacted and are working with us.")

- Provide whatever follow-up information is available. ("The school was searched by the police and no bomb was found. A suspect has been identified.")

- Make yourself available. ("Call us if you have any questions or concerns.") In our experience, such letters have been well received and have not generated a rash of phone calls or parent complaints.

RECORD KEEPING

Are the notes from my threat assessment part of the student's record? The answer to this question depends on how school personnel choose to maintain and use the notes they make in conducting a threat assessment. According to FERPA (1974), private notes are not part of the student's educational record. However, the FERPA definition of private notes is fairly stringent. Notes must be kept in the sole possession of the maker and "not accessible or revealed to any other person except a temporary substitute for the maker of the record." If the notes are routinely shared with others, they would be considered part of the student's record. And, of course, even private notes can be subpoenaed by a court of law.

What do I put in the student's file? Schools should follow their existing policy regarding discipline violations. Every threat of violence should constitute some form of discipline infraction that can be recorded according to school policy. Even transient threats often involve a disciplinary violation. In very serious substantive cases, schools should prepare a written safety plan or report that is placed in the confidential section of the student's file. This report documents the school's efforts to maintain safety and also provides valuable information in the event of future threats or violent acts.

What should I do when a student who made a threat is returning to school after a suspension? If a student has made a threat that resulted in a lengthy school suspension, there may be some concern among other students or parents when that student returns to school. Because the situation is no longer an emergency and undoubtedly the incident has become a part of the student's records, you must be more cautious in what information you disclose to others. From a safety perspective, it is still legitimate to share information with other school staff. The student who is returning to school may merit close observation, and this student may become the target of hostility from other students. Although there is no known case law on this point, it is appropriate to notify parents of victims when a student who made a threat is returning to school. The fact that a student is returning to school is not a confidential matter because it is a public event. In anticipation of a student's return to school, it is advisable to obtain permission from the student's parents to notify the person or persons who were threatened (see the preceding parent notification section).

SCHOOL RESOURCE OFFICERS

What if my school does not have an SRO? Many schools do not have school resource officers. In these cases, the school should consult with the local police department and, if possible, identify a liaison officer. School administrators should develop a good working relationship with the local police department and clarify the circumstances in which it would be appropriate to contact the police.

Do I have to contact the school resource officer if a student makes a violent threat? Some states have enacted laws requiring school administrators to report criminal acts to law enforcement, so schools should check the laws for their state. For example, Virginia law (Code of Virginia, 2000) requires the principal to report to law enforcement authorities any act that may constitute assault or assault and battery; sexual assault; death, shooting, cutting, stabbing, or other wounding; use, possession, or distribution of alcohol, a controlled substance, or an imitation controlled substance; threats against school personnel; explosive or incendiary devices; and use or possession of a firearm.

In general, it is not necessary to contact law enforcement if a student makes a transient threat, unless the threat involves a clear legal violation, such as a bomb threat. However, school administrators may want to consult with an SRO even for less serious threats, so that the SRO is informed about school events and will be alert to rumors that may circulate about the incident. In addition, it may be appropriate for the SRO to speak with a student who is in the habit of making threatening statements.

Substantive threats of violence are potentially dangerous situations and can be violations of law, so it would be good practice to consult with the SRO. In emergency or crisis situations, the school administrator should call 911 and follow the school's crisis response plan.

What will the school resource officer do about a substantive threat? In most cases, the student will not be arrested, but the officer may wish to speak with the student or observe an interview with the principal. Officers are trained to use their judgment in making an arrest, considering the overall situation, including the student's age, behavior, and response to authority. Principals should discuss arrest policies with their SROs at the beginning of the school year.

What if a student refuses to cooperate with the investigation of a violent threat? School officials and the police are permitted to detain and question a student who is thought to be planning an act of violence at school, according to a 2000 federal court ruling (*Milligan v. City of Slidell*, 2000). The court reasoned that the school's

obligation to protect others takes precedence over the student's right to privacy.

What if I find that a student has an illegal drug in his or her possession? Students in possession of illegal drugs must be reported immediately to the SRO or the police department. If school personnel keep the illegal substance in their possession, they are subject to arrest.

SEARCHES

Can I search a student who has made a violent threat? Yes, you can search a student, the student's belongings, and the student's locker if you are concerned that the student has a weapon or some other means of harming others. You may also search for evidence that a student is planning to harm someone, for example, if you have reasonable suspicion that the student has prepared a written plan or "hit list."

The Fourth Amendment to the U.S. Constitution guarantees "the right of the people to be secure in their persons, houses, papers, and effects, against unreasonable searches and seizures." Before 1985, doubt existed about whether this right applied to students in the public schools. Schools argued that administrators acted in loco parentis—in the place of the parent—while students were at school. In 1985, the U.S. Supreme Court determined that the Fourth Amendment applies to students in the public schools (*New Jersey v. T.L.O.*). In this case the court ruled that school officials have special authority to keep schools safe and therefore are not required to obtain search warrants or use the standard of probable cause like police officers. School officials can act based on "reasonable suspicion." This standard gives school officials considerable authority to use their own professional judgment about what is appropriate to do in order to maintain a safe and orderly school environment, in keeping with the educational mission of the school. School officials can conduct a search "where there are reasonable grounds for suspecting that the search will turn up evidence that the student has violated or is violating either the law or the rules of the school."

Can I ask the school resource officer to search a student or the student's locker?

Police officers, including SROs, can initiate a search only with probable cause, which is a higher standard set by the U.S. Supreme Court in a series of decisions. Probable cause to search exists when "known facts and circumstances are sufficient to warrant a man of reasonable prudence in the belief that contraband . . . will be found" (*Ornelas v. United States*, 1996, at 696).

Educators, on the other hand, can search a locker if they have cause for *reasonable suspicion*, which is a less stringent standard. According to U.S. Supreme Court standards, reasonable suspicion is satisfied when two conditions exist: (1) the search is justified at its inception, meaning that there are reasonable grounds for suspecting that the search will reveal evidence that the student has violated or is violating the law or school rules; and (2) the search is reasonably related in scope to the circumstances that justified the search, meaning that the measures used to conduct the search are reasonably related to the objectives of the search and that the search is not excessively intrusive in light of the student's age and sex and the nature of the offense.

New Jersey v. T.L.O. (1985) is the most important U.S. Supreme Court case on student searches. Because the standard is less stringent for educators, it is often best if school personnel conduct the search with the SRO in an observing role. The SRO can become involved if evidence is uncovered that meets the standard of probable cause.

The SRO can also become involved if the school staff member has concerns about immediate personal safety or the safety of others in conducting the search and asks the SRO for assistance for this reason. For example, if a school administrator is concerned that a student may become aggressive during a search, the administrator can ask the SRO for assistance. In such cases where safety is the primary concern, some courts have allowed the SRO to become involved in assisting the educator and to search

the student. See *State of Wisconsin v. Angelia D. B.* (1997) and *K. K. v. State of Florida* (1998).

What about strip searches? In almost all cases, the answer is, "Don't do them." Strip searches should be conducted only in dire circumstances. Such searches should not be conducted for the purpose of finding contraband, notes, money, or other nondangerous items. Consult your state's Department of Education regulations for more guidance.

SPECIAL EDUCATION

What if a student in special education makes a threat?

School staff should conduct threat assessments regardless of the student's special education status. The safety of students and staff is the top priority, and so, in an emergency situation, school authorities should proceed with the steps that seem necessary and appropriate to prevent an act of violence. Once immediate safety has been addressed, school authorities must also consider issues related to special education law. A student with a disability is entitled to a free, appropriate education in the least restrictive environment, as described in the Individuals with Disabilities Education Act (IDEA) of 1997. The 2004 revision of this act (IDEA 2004) is the binding federal law, effective July 2005. Federal regulations delineating procedures and requirements for meeting IDEA 2004 will be released at a later date. For new information, check with your local special education department. Web sites with helpful information include www.wrightslaw.org, www.findlaw.org, and www.pent.ca.gov.

Can schools suspend a student in special education who makes a threat?

Yes, but a school suspension in some circumstances can be regarded as a change in the student's educational placement. The following conditions apply:

- If the student will not have accrued more than ten days of suspension in a school year, including this suspension, then there are no additional special requirements. Discipline may proceed the same as for students without special education eligibility.

- If the suspension will bring the student's total days of suspension to more than 10 days in the school year, IDEA '97 requires specific actions to ensure that the student continues to receive free and appropriate education. It is anticipated that the forthcoming federal regulations for IDEA 2004 will maintain the process described here. Current federal regulations require the school administrator to take actions to ensure that the student is continuing to make progress in the general education core curriculum as well as meeting individual goals listed on the IEP during the suspension. These provisions are legally required to prevent a suspension from becoming a de facto change in placement occurring outside the mandated IEP team process. Typically a suspension is for only a brief time, and services can be provided to ensure necessary progress. (Forms to help you adhere to this provision are available at www.pent.ca.gov). If the suspension leads to an accrual of more than 10 days in a school year, a functional behavioral assessment is required (O'Neill et al.,1997; Nelson, Roberts, & Smith, 1998). If the IEP team determines that the student needs a change in placement and the student's parent agrees with this change in placement, the change can be made. If an involuntary change in placement or expulsion is considered, the IEP team must also conduct a manifestation determination review before moving to expulsion or any involuntary change in placement (described in the following section).

- If the principal determines that a weapon or drugs were involved in the threat or that the student is dangerous, then the student can be placed in an interim alternative placement for 45 days without parent permission. During this time period, the school must conduct all required processes, including a functional behavioral assessment and development of a behavior intervention plan, a manifestation determination, and all necessary meetings and hearings with the parents to resolve any conflicts over recommendations. If the IEP team determines that an immediate change in placement is required and the parent gives informed consent to that change in placement, the 45-day interim alternative placement is not required. The 45-day limit applies only for involuntary changes in school placement when the student's removal is due to weapons, drugs, or dangerousness.

What is a manifestation determination?

If a student is eligible for special education services, then changes in school placement are governed by special education law. Ordinarily, the parents must give informed consent for a change in placement. If the parents do not give informed consent for a change in placement, the IEP team must hold a manifestation determination IEP meeting. Under IDEA '97, a manifestation determination meeting must make four determinations: (1) that at the time of the threatening behavior, the IEP was appropriate; (2) that at the time of the threatening behavior, all necessary supplementary aids and supports were being provided as specified in the IEP; (3) that the student understood the impact and outcome of the behavior; and (4) that the student could control the behavior. If all four determinations are made, the student may be expelled or assigned to an involuntary placement. If any of the four determinations are not made, neither expulsion nor involuntary placement is permitted, and the student's IEP team must determine appropriate placement and services (see Chapter 10 for more information). IDEA 2004 states that the behavior must be directly related to the disability and does not use the full four-point decision guide listed in IDEA '97. However, the federal regulations to implement IDEA 2004 may restore this guide or provide other clarification of the criteria for manifestation determination.

How do you determine whether a student's threat is a manifestation of the student's disability? It is sometimes difficult to determine whether or not a student's disability affected his or her ability to understand the impact and outcome of the behavior and whether or not he or she could control the behavior. Under IDEA 2004, a student's threat must be directly related to the disability, but the regulations explaining how to determine this have not been released. This is an issue that is in need of both scientific research and further legal guidance. Nevertheless, some cases are relatively clear-cut. For example, if a student with an emotional disturbance has auditory hallucinations that direct him or her to threaten someone or if the student has the delusional belief that he or she is endangered by another student, then it is reasonable for the IEP team to conclude that the student either did not understand the impact and outcome of the behavior or was unable to control the behavior. Under these circumstances, it also seems reasonable to conclude that the student's threat was directly related to his or her disability. If a student has mental retardation that precludes adequate use of logical reasoning, the IEP team also may conclude that the student lacked sufficient understanding of the impact and outcome of the behavior. If a student has a less severe emotional disturbance or some other disability such as a learning disability, it is much more likely that he or she would be able to understand the impact and outcome of the behavior or be able to control the behavior. Because the determination that a behavior is directly related to a disability is subject to varied interpretation, threatening behavior must be considered on a case-by-case basis.

It is important to keep in mind that the manifestation determination is an IEP team process that goes beyond examining the connection between the disability and the threatening behavior. The IEP team must assess whether the IEP in place at the time of the threat was appropriate and working effectively. If a problem behavior is occurring repeatedly, there should have been a plan in place to address it. It is common for a manifestation determination to hinge on the finding that the IEP plan failed to provide an appropriate placement or lacked adequate provision of all necessary supplementary aids and supports—because the behavior was an ongoing problem that was not properly addressed. A behavior plan is considered a supplementary support that the student needed to address the problem behavior. If the threat was a one-time event, then the IEP team is likely to conclude that placement and supports were adequate. If these conditions are met, the IEP team will need to apply the current federal law and regulations. Until new federal regulations are released, the 1997 regulations direct the IEP team to consider two critical questions regarding the link between the threat and the disability: "As a result of the disability, is the student unable to understand the impact and outcome of the behavior?" and "As a result of the disability, is the student unable to control the behavior?" Teams are cautioned to update their procedures when new federal regulations are released and to keep in mind that there may be additional changes in state law and regulations, as well as new court decisions, that affect these procedures.

What if a threat is a manifestation of the student's disability? Can a student be kept out of school if we do not feel it is safe to have him or her in school? Safety is always the top priority. If the school administration concludes that it is not safe for a student to attend the current school, the student should not be allowed to return. However, there should be clear indication that there is no safe alternative solution, such as the IEP team developing a behavior plan that provides the student with adequate support to attend school safely. If the student has special education eligibility and does not meet the current legal requirements for a manifestation determination (see previous question), the school district must design an IEP with an appropriate placement and expulsion cannot occur.

IDEA '97 allowed involuntary interim alternative placements of up to 45 calendar days and provided for extensions of that provision by a hearing officer if the student is found to be dangerous by a preponderance of evidence. The conditions and length of alternative placements may be modified by the forthcoming regulations for IDEA 2004.

It is always important to remember that the IEP team can change a student's placement if the parent agrees with the change. If the parent does not agree with the change in placement, the IEP team is obligated to proceed with all necessary special education mediation or hearing steps to determine what constitutes an appropriate education in the least restrictive environment. The IEP team must present its reasons why the proposed placement change is necessary to provide the student with a free and appropriate public education in the least restrictive environment. Federal and state laws and regulations governing special education are complex; school administrators are advised to consult their legal counsel for current requirements and practices.

TYPES OF THREATS

Both threats made in jest and threats that express genuine anger can be considered transient threats, but aren't they different types of threats? Is a joke really a threat at all? The category of transient threats includes a variety of threatening behaviors that could be subclassified. Statements that are merely figures of speech or joking comments that do not convey real hostility toward someone could be classified as "nonthreats" or "false threats." However, we judged that such a system would be more complex than is necessary or practical in everyday use. We grouped all threats that did not require protective action—either because they were based on a misunderstanding of the student's behavior or because the student's threat was readily resolved—into the same category. If research or practice demonstrates the value of further subclassification of threats, this approach can be revised.

What if a student has not made a threat but appears to be dangerous? Can I do a threat assessment anyway? If a student appears to be dangerous, it is important to consider carefully what behaviors or signs indicate

dangerousness, in order to avoid the pitfalls of profiling or stereotyping students. In some cases, it may be useful to meet with a student and inquire about his or her concerns and intentions. In other cases where there is strong concern about a student—perhaps because of a history of aggressive behavior—it would be reasonable to conduct a modified threat assessment.

What if I am unsure whether a threat is transient or substantive and so begin the process of treating the threat as substantive but later determine that it is transient? If you are uncertain whether a threat is transient or substantive, it is safest to investigate the threat as substantive. This situation occurs most often when the student who made the threat is unavailable for interview after the threat has been reported and school authorities feel compelled to take protective action. For example, a student might have sent a threatening letter to someone, but the student is not in school to be interviewed. If subsequent investigation determines that a threat is actually transient (e.g., the student's threatening letter was a prank), then the threat can be reclassified as transient and further investigation can be stopped.

ZERO TOLERANCE

Doesn't the federal law on gun-free schools require automatic expulsion anytime a student brings a weapon to school? No. Both the original Gun-Free Schools Act of 1994 (1994) and the newer language that is part of the No Child Left Behind Act of 2001 (2002) permit schools to exercise judgment and make exceptions to the expulsion requirement on a case-by-case basis. According to the revisions of the Gun-Free Schools Act of 1994, which was reauthorized by the No Child Left Behind Act of 2001:

> Each state . . . shall have in effect a state law requiring [schools] to expel from school for a period of not less than one year a student who is determined to have brought a firearm to school or to have possessed a firearm at a school . . . except that such state law shall

allow the chief administering officer of such local educational agency to modify such expulsion requirement for a student on a case-by-case basis if such modification is in writing. (§ 4141)

Doesn't the law require that I treat all firearms, including pellet guns and BB guns, the same as regular handguns and rifles? This is a common error. According to the Gun-Free Schools Act, the definition of a firearm "does not apply to items such as toy guns, cap guns, bb guns, and pellet guns" (U.S. Department of Education, Office of Safe and Drug-Free Schools, 2003, p. 141).

Moreover, the law does not even apply to all firearms. Section 4141 (g) of the Gun-Free Schools Act states that the law does *not* "apply to a firearm that is lawfully stored inside a locked vehicle on school property, or if it is for activities approved and authorized by the local educational agency and the local educational agency adopts appropriate safeguards to ensure student safety."

CHAPTER 8

RESEARCH

FINDINGS

These guidelines were field tested in two school divisions during the 2001–2002 school year. The purpose of the field test was to demonstrate that school-based teams could be trained to carry out threat assessment in a safe, efficient, and effective manner. Secondarily, the study measured the frequency of transient and substantive cases and investigated the consequences of those different types of threats. Some of the research findings in this chapter are reported elsewhere (Cornell, 2003; Cornell, Sheras, Kaplan, McConville, et al., 2004; Cornell & Williams, in press).

RESEARCH SITES

The two school divisions consisted of four high schools (grades 9–12), six middle schools (grades 6–8), 22 elementary schools (kindergarten–grade 5), and three alternative schools (grades 7–12), serving a population of 129,000 in a single county in central Virginia. The county covers 736 square miles and includes urban, suburban, and rural areas. The combined enrollment of the two school divisions was 16,273 students, of which 71% were Caucasian, 22% African American, and 7% other groups. Approximately 26% of the students were eligible for free or reduced-price meals.

DATA COLLECTION

School principals reported cases by completing an electronic form at a secure Web site. This form served the dual purpose of providing schools with printed documentation of their response to a student threat and informing researchers of a new case. The Web site form collected demographic information (age, gender, grade, and race) about the student who made the threat and the intended threat victim, provided space for a description of the threat incident, and presented a checklist of actions taken in response to the threat (e.g., suspending or expelling the student, assigning detention, and contacting police).

A graduate student research liaison was assigned to each school; the liaison remained in contact with the school principals over the course of the school year and conducted face-to-face follow-up interviews to collect additional case information. Follow-up interviews were conducted for each case on two occasions, during the final weeks of the school year and again the following fall. The average follow-up period from the date of the threat incident to the principal interview at the end of the school year was 148 days (range 3 to 282 days). The second follow-up interview occurred an average of 424 days after the threat incident.

WHO MADE THREATS?

A total of 188 cases of student threats were reported by school principals (or assistant principals) during the 2001–2002 school year. These cases included threats made by 86 elementary school, 61 middle school, and 41 high school students. As indicated in *Figure 4*, threats were observed at each grade level from kindergarten to twelfth grade. The students making the threats were identified as Caucasian (54.8%), African American (43.1%), or Hispanic (1.1%). The percentage of students of African American ancestry who were identified as making threats (43.1%) is almost double their representation in school enrollment (22%) and requires further investigation. Disproportionate minority representation is a common finding in studies of school discipline outcomes (Skiba, Michael, Nardo, & Peterson, 2000). Fifty-one percent of the students identified as making threats were eligible for free or reduced-price school meals. In 16 cases, a student made more than one threat, but for the purposes of this study, each threat incident was treated as a separate case.

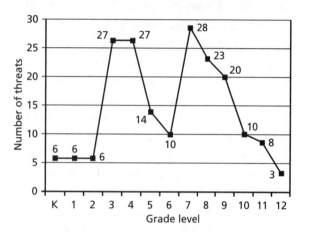

Figure 4. **Threats reported at each grade level**

WHO REPORTED THE THREATS?

Most threats were reported by teachers and students (see *Figure 5*). A smaller number were reported by parents, school administrators (including counselors), or others (e.g., a bus driver). Most threats were reported soon after they were observed, but in some cases the threat

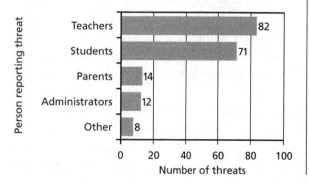

Figure 5. **Persons reporting student threats**

was reported a day or more later. For example, a student might go home and tell his parents that he had been threatened, prompting one of the parents to call the principal the next day. Threats were reported to the school principal, who then initiated the first step in the threat assessment.

WHERE DID THE THREATS OCCUR?

Threats most often took place in the classroom. Students spend the majority of their time in the classroom, and therefore they are the most likely places where a threat would be observed by a teacher or other adult. Nevertheless, threats occurred in almost every conceivable location, including the hallways and outside of the building, at the bus stop, and in the cafeteria, gym, and restrooms (see *Figure 6*).

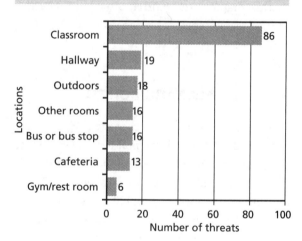

Figure 6. **Threat locations**

It is important to recognize that many other threats may have occurred that were not reported to school authorities and so were not subject to threat assessment. In those cases, the students observing the threats may have judged that the threats were not serious and so did not report them. In other cases, such as bullying, the threatened student may have been reluctant to seek help because of a belief that nothing would or could be done to stop the bullying (Unnever & Cornell, 2003). The prevalence of student threats is a little-studied topic, although anonymous self-report studies suggest that student threats of violence occur with surprising frequency. Cornell and Loper (1998) reported results from a survey of 10,909 students (grades 7, 9, and 11) in which more than one fourth of students replied "yes" to the item "someone threatened to hurt you at school" in the past 30 days. Singer and Flannery (2000) found that more than 10% of students reported threatening someone frequently ("often" or "almost every day"). These findings suggest that students make far more threats of violence than are reported to school authorities. In a school population of 16,273, if just 10% of students made a threat at school every month, one could expect more than 14,600 threats over the course of the school year. Clearly, the epidemiology of student threats is an area for further study.

WHO DID STUDENTS THREATEN?

Students usually threatened other students (141 of 188, or 75% of cases), but there were nearly two dozen threats against teachers and eight threats against other persons such as school administrators. In 17 cases, there were multiple threat recipients, including some cases with no specific victims (e.g., "I'm going to blow up the school") (see *Figure 7*).

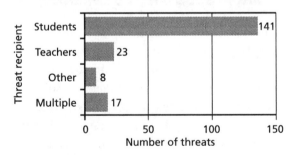

Figure 7. **Threat recipient or victim**

In the 143 cases of a student threatening another student, the students tended to be in the same grade; there were 21 cases in which a student threatened a student in a lower grade, 105 threats of students in the same grade, and 15 threats of students in a higher grade.

Gender and race analyses are reported in *Table 1*. There were 146 threats made by boys and 42 by girls. Excluding 22 cases in which a student threatened both a male and a female

victim, students tended to threaten persons of the same sex. In 84 cases (51%), boys threatened other males; in 44 cases (27%), boys threatened females; in 22 cases (13%), girls threatened other females; and in 16 cases (10%), girls threatened males. Gender concordance was 64% ($\kappa = .19$, $p < .01$).

Table 1. **Gender and race concordance**

Perpetrator	Victim		χ^2	κ
Gender	Male	Female	8.33*	.19*
Male	84	44		
Female	16	22		
Race	Caucasian	Minority	33.72**	.40**
Caucasian	76	16		
Minority	34	42		

* $p < .01$. ** $p < .001$.

There were 103 threats made by Caucasian students and 85 by non-Caucasian or minority students. Excluding 20 cases in which a student threatened victims of multiple races, students tended to threaten persons of the same race category (70%) ($\kappa = .40$, $p < .001$). In 76 cases (45%), Caucasian students threatened other Caucasians; in 16 cases (10%), Caucasians threatened minority students; in 42 cases (25%), minority students threatened other minority students; and in 34 cases (20%), minority students threatened Caucasians.

WHAT DID THE STUDENTS THREATEN TO DO?

The most common threat was to hit or beat up the victim (77 cases, or 41%). In addition, there were 27 threats to kill, 24 threats to shoot, and 18 threats to cut or stab. There were 32 cases in which the threat was vague or nonspecific ("I'm going to get you") and 10 miscellaneous other threats, such as setting fires or detonating bombs (see *Figure 8*).

Table 2 presents a breakdown of threats at the elementary, middle, and high school levels.

Figure 8. **Types of student threats**

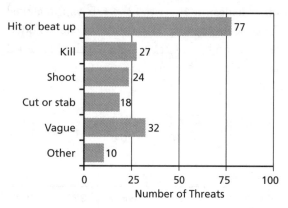

All types of threats were seen at all school levels. Threats to kill and threats to shoot actually occurred more frequently in elementary school than in middle and high school combined. This observation strengthened our view that the content of the threat alone is not especially helpful in determining the seriousness of the threat.

Table 2. **Types of threats by school level**

School level	Threatened behavior						
	Hit	Kill	Shoot	Stab	Vague	Other	Total
Elementary	34	17	13	9	9	4	86
Middle	23	8	8	4	15	3	61
High	20	2	3	5	8	3	41
Total	77	27	24	18	32	10	188

HOW WERE THE THREATS CLASSIFIED?

The majority (70%) of threats were classified as transient threats. Of the remaining 30% that were classified as substantive threats, 22% (42 cases) were serious substantive threats and 8% (15 cases) were very serious substantive threats (see *Figure 9*).

Using school enrollment data, we calculated the rate of threats per 1,000 students for elementary, middle, and high schools. Because some schools did not begin collecting data until several weeks into the school year, annual threat rates were extrapolated for each school. For transient threats, the rate per 1,000 students was 11.3 (90% confidence interval, 9.2 to 13.9) for

Figure 9. **Breakdown of threat types**

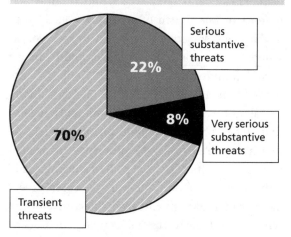

elementary school, 12.1 (8.8 to 16.2) for middle school, and 6.7 (4.8 to 9.5) for high school.

For substantive threats, the rate per 1,000 students was 2.1 (90% confidence interval, 1.3 to 3.4) for elementary school, 7.96 (5.4 to 11.4) for middle school, and 4.3 (2.8 to 6.5) for high school. We caution that threat rates varied from school to school and are dependent on many factors, including the willingness of students to report threats and the degree of monitoring and supervision provided by school staff.

HOW DID TRANSIENT THREATS DIFFER FROM SUBSTANTIVE THREATS?

Distinct grade trends emerged when threats were classified as transient or substantive (see *Figure 10*). Transient threats were most frequent in third and fourth grades. We observed that many of these cases involved students engaged in peer disputes such as who was going to be best friends with whom. Students with hurt feelings sometimes made verbal threats, or even wrote threatening letters, that resulted in a disciplinary referral and threat assessment. In contrast, substantive threats appeared to peak in middle school, particularly in grades 7 and 8, and did not decline until after grade 9, the first grade of high school. A chi-square test comparing elementary, middle, and high schools in type of threat was statistically significant, x^2 (1, $N = 188$) = 16.41 ($p < .001$; contingency coefficient $C = .28$). At the elementary school level, only 15% (13 of 86) of threats were substantive, whereas at the middle and high school levels, the proportion of substantive threats was much higher, being 41% (25 of 61) and 44% (18 of 41), respectively.

Figure 10. **Transient and substantive threats for each grade level**

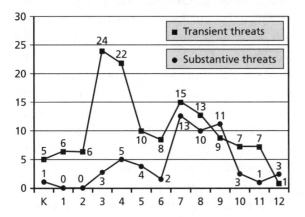

The association between type of threat (transient versus substantive) and student gender and race was considered. Male students made the majority of both transient (104 of 132, or 79%) and substantive (42 of 56, or 75%) threats, and the association between gender and threat type was not statistically significant, x^2 (1, $N = 188$) = .33 ($p = .57$). Minority students made 51% (67 of 132) of transient threats and 41% (23 of 56) of substantive threats, but again the difference was not statistically significant, x^2 (1, $N = 188$) = 1.48 ($p = .22$).

Males were recipients of 60% (73 of 121) of transient threats and 60% (27 of 45) of substantive threats, x^2 (1, $N = 166$) = .01 ($p = .97$). (The N was 166 because some cases involved both male and female victims.) Minority students were recipients of 40% (53 of 132) of transient threats and 45% (25 of 56) of substantive threats, x^2 (1, $N = 188$) = .33 ($p = .57$).

Finally, the association between the type of threat and threat content, i.e., what the student threatened to do, was examined (see *Figure 11*). As expected, threat content was unrelated to type of threat, x^2 (5, $N = 188$) = 8.27 ($p = .14$). It is instructive to observe that nearly all threats to kill someone were found to be transient threats.

Figure 11. **Relation of threat content to threat type**

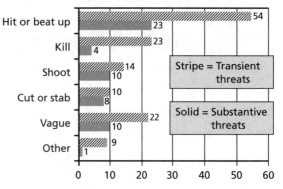

The statistically nonsignificant findings for gender, race, and threat content can be regarded as positive results, because they suggest that school personnel were not biased by these factors. Presumably, they were making judgments based on the context and meaning of the student's threat.

WHAT WERE THE DISCIPLINARY CONSEQUENCES FOR THREATS?

Only 3 of the 188 threat cases resulted in expulsion from school. One case was a sixth grade boy who was expelled after picking up a pair of scissors and threatening to stab a classmate. A second case was an eighth grade girl who was expelled after telling a classmate that she was going to shoot him. The third case was a ninth grade girl who was expelled after threatening to stab another student and subsequently was found to have a knife in her locker. In each case, school authorities considered the student's prior discipline infractions as decisive in the expulsion. The three students had a combined total of 53 disciplinary infractions for the school year.

School suspension was a frequent consequence for a threat (see *Figure 12*). Fully half (94 cases) of the students who made threats were given a short-term suspension from school. The modal suspension (32 cases) was 1 day, with a range of 1 to 10 days. Only 12 students were placed in an alternative educational setting. Like the decision to expel a student, this decision was based on careful consideration of the student's disciplinary history.

These students had an average of 9.8 disciplinary infractions for the school year.

It is noteworthy that only six students were arrested after making a threat. In each case, the

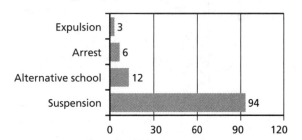

Figure 12. **Threat consequences**

school resource officer judged that the student's behavior warranted an arrest. Three of the arrests were made after the student made a false bomb threat. Two students were arrested because they assaulted a school staff member and had to be restrained. The final case involved the ninth grade girl (noted previously) who had a knife in her locker.

Finally, disciplinary consequences for transient and substantive cases were compared. All three students who were expelled from school made substantive threats. Students who made substantive threats (45 of 56 cases, or 80%) were more likely to be suspended from school than were students who made transient threats (49 of 132 cases, or 37%), x^2 (1, $N = 188$) = 29.40 ($p < .001$, $C = .37$). Students who made transient threats (22 of 132 cases, or 17%) were more likely to receive an in-school detention or time-out than students who made substantive threats (3 of 56 cases, or 5%), x^2 (1, $N = 188$) = 4.36 ($p = .037$, $C = .15$). Students who made transient threats (16 of 132 cases, or 12%) received more after-school detentions than students who made substantive threats (2 of 54 cases, or 4%), but the difference was not statistically significant, x^2 (1, $N = 188$) = 3.32 ($p = .07$).

WHAT HAPPENED AFTER THE THREAT?

At the end of the school year, principals were interviewed to obtain follow-up information on each threat case in their school. In order to extend the follow-up period, each principal was interviewed a second time the following fall. Because of Institutional Review Board restrictions, no effort was made to contact students involved in the threats. School principals were asked three basic questions: (1) How has the student's behavior changed since the threat assessment? (2) How has the student's relationship with the threat recipient changed? (3) Did the student carry out the threatened act of violence? In some cases, the principal did not feel he or she had sufficient information to answer the question (for example, if the student left school).

In most cases ($n = 176$), the student's behavior was rated as improved (43%) or the same (39%), and in only 18% of cases did the student's behavior worsen. Principals rated the student's relationship with the threat recipient in 126 cases (excluding cases in which the principal did not feel sufficiently informed or the student did not threaten a specific individual). In nearly two thirds (63%) of cases, the relationship was judged to be the same; in about one third (32%) of cases, it was improved; and in only 6 cases (5%) was it judged to be worse (see *Figure 13*).

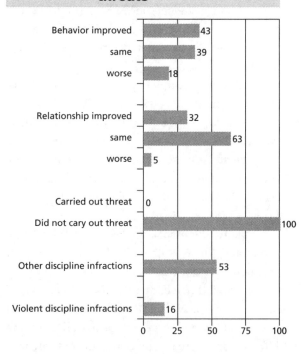

Figure 13. **Follow-up on student threats**

Perhaps the most critical question was whether the student carried out the threatened act of violence. According to the principals, none of the threats were carried out. (Data were available for 185 student threats; in 3 cases, the principal was not sure whether a student's threat to hit another student was carried out.) Nevertheless, many of the students continued to have discipline problems. More than half (53%) of the students had a subsequent disciplinary violation of some kind, and 16% had a disciplinary violation that involved violent or aggressive behavior such as hitting someone or getting into a fight.

HOW DID TRANSIENT AND SUBSTANTIVE CASES COMPARE AT FOLLOW-UP?

These analyses investigated whether students judged to have made transient threats had better outcomes than students judged to have made substantive threats. As expected, the ratings indicated more positive behavior for students who made transient threats (51 improved, 57 same, 16 worse) than for the students who made substantive threats (25 improved, 12 same, 15 worse), x^2 $(1, N = 176) = 10.59$ $(p = .005, C = .24)$. Similarly, when principals rated the student's relationship with the threat recipient, the ratings for transient cases (31 improved, 57 same, 1 worse) were more positive than those for substantive cases (9 improved, 23 same, 5 worse), x^2 $(1, N = 126) = 9.35$ $(p = .009, C = .26)$. These results are presented in *Figure 14* with

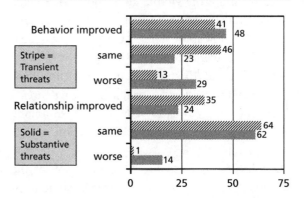

Figure 14. **Outcomes for transient and substantive threats**

percentages rather than raw frequencies to assist in interpretation.

HOW ARE THREATS RELATED TO SPECIAL EDUCATION ELIGIBILITY?

One of the most complex issues in student threat assessment concerns students receiving special education services. How does special education eligibility affect a threat assessment, and what procedural modifications should be considered when a student is disabled? To gather information that can be used to address such questions, a series of analyses compared threats made by students in general programs and in special education programs.

Students with special education eligibility made a disproportionate number of threats. As shown in *Table 3*, the rate of threats made by these students (33 per 1,000 students) was much higher than that for students placed solely in general education classrooms (6.9 per 1,000 students), $x^2 = 142.1$ $(p < .001, C = .71)$. Among all students with special education eligibility, students with emotionally disabled (ED) status made the most threats, despite their relatively small numbers. The threat rate for students with ED status (210 per 1,000) was far higher than that for students receiving services for learning disabilities (LD) (28 per 1,000) or other health impairments (OHI) (45 per 1,000), $x^2 = 126.08$ $(p < .001, C = .87)$. One observation about the OHI group: Although OHI is a broad category that in principle could encompass many different disorders, all of the students identified for services under this category carried a diagnosis of attention deficit disorder.

The proportion of transient versus substantive threats made by students in general education versus those made by students with special education eligibility was examined. Of the 95 threats by students in the general education group, 18% were judged to be substantive by the threat assessment team leader. In contrast, of the 93 threats by students in the special education group, 40% were judged to be substantive. The association between special education status and type of threat was statistically significant,

Table 3. Threat rates for students in general versus special education programs

Classification	School enrollment	Number of threats	Rate per 1,000 students
General education	13,612	95	6.9
Special education	2,788	93	33
ED	271	57	210
LD	1,028	29	28
OHI	399	18	45

x^2 (1, N = 188) = 10.57 (p < .01, C = .23). These findings indicate that school administrators are more likely to regard a threat by a student eligible for special education as a serious threat requiring protective action. Further research is needed to identify the factors associated with these students that would explain this finding. Anecdotal observations suggest that it is possible that the students in the special education group who made threats had a history of aggressive behavior or were less cooperative in the threat assessment, so that their threats were regarded more seriously. School administrators may have been more uncertain about the likelihood that a student with special education status would carry out a threat, and hence they were more likely to classify the threat as substantive.

HOW DO THREATS BY STUDENTS ELIGIBLE FOR SPECIAL EDUCATION SERVICES COMPARE WITH THREATS BY STUDENTS SOLELY IN GENERAL EDUCATION CLASSES?

This question was addressed with a series of comparisons.

Perpetrator and victim status. As shown in *Table 4*, general education students rarely threatened students in special education; however, students in special education threatened both general education and special education students.

Out of the total 188 threats made, 33 cases were excluded because education status was not known for the perpetrator or the victim. In the 155 cases where the classification was known, students in general education classes almost always threatened other students in general education classes (95%, or 76 out of 80 threats). Students receiving special education services made threats against other students receiving special education services 73% of the time (55 out of 75 threats), and 27% of their threats were against students in general education (20 out of 75 threats).

Table 4. Perpetrator versus target education classification

Perpetrator	Target		
	General education	Special education	Total
General education	76	4	80
Special education	55	20	75

Type of threat. Next, differences in the types of threats made by students in special education versus students in general education were considered; however, the comparison was not statistically significant, x^2 (1, N = 188) = 1.92 (p = .93, C = .23). The most common threat for both groups was to hit or beat up the victim; of the 77 cases of this nature, 40 were made by students in general education and 37 by students in special education. Of the 27 threats to kill, 14 were made by students in general education and 13 by students in special education. A total of 24 threats were to shoot the victim; 10 of those were made by general education students and 14 by students in special education. The 18 threats to cut or stab the victim were made by 8 students in general education and 10 students in special education. The remaining 42 vague or miscellaneous threats were also approximately equally divided among students in general and special education.

Disciplinary outcome. A comparison of the disciplinary consequences received by students in general and special education programs showed only minor differences in the three most severe outcomes of threats by each group of students. Of the three threats resulting in expulsion, one was made by a student in general education, and two were made by students in special education. Two students in general education were arrested, compared with four students in special education. Similarly, five students in general education and seven in special education received placement in an alternative school. Looking more closely at the most common discipline outcome of suspension, however, students in special education were suspended significantly more often than students in general education, x^2 (1, N = 186) = 13.88 ($p < .05$, $C = .26$), as seen in *Table 5*. Also, the length of the suspension was significantly greater for students in special education. Note that a separate analysis of a larger sample of cases by Kaplan (2005) did not find statistically significant differences in suspensions between students receiving general education services and those receiving special education services.

Table 5. **General versus special education suspension days**

Classification	Suspended		x^2
	No	Yes	13.88*
General education	54	41	
Special education	40	51	

Follow-up status. Two analyses investigated whether students in general education had better outcomes than students in special education. Ratings indicated more positive behavior for students in general education (47 improved, 35 same, 7 worse) than that for students in special education (29 improved, 34 same, 24 worse), x^2 (1, N = 176) = 13.58 ($p = .001$, $C = .27$). Similarly, more students in general education were reported as having no disciplinary infractions following the threat (82 no, 13 yes) in comparison with students in special education (68 no, 25 yes), x^2

(1, N = 188) = 5.08 ($p = .024$, $C = .16$). These results are presented in *Figure 15*.

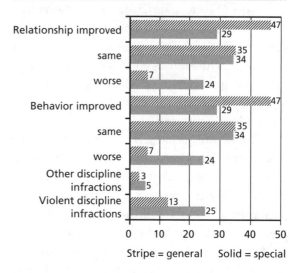

Figure 15. **Outcomes for perpetrators in general and special education**

WHAT FURTHER RESEARCH IS NEEDED?

The research findings reported here are from a field-test study and not an experimental comparison among different approaches to student threats. A comparison group to assess how threats would have been resolved using another method would be necessary in order to demonstrate that the student outcomes in this study were a specific result of the threat assessment approach. A formal comparison with one or more alternative methods would be an appropriate next step, now that the threat assessment model has been devised and field tested.

Nevertheless, it is noteworthy that these schools, using a threat assessment approach, had such positive results. First of all, none of the threats was carried out, which is a finding that would match or exceed the outcome from any other approach. Additional research is needed, however, to assess how frequently student threats are carried out, in order to determine an expected base rate for different kinds of threats. Presumably, most threats that students make are not carried out, but it may require a much larger sample of threats to determine such rates. In any case, these results should be reassuring to school administrators who are faced with a student threat and concerned that the student will harm someone.

Second, almost all of the students were able to return to school. Only 3 students were expelled, 12 students were transferred to an alternative school, and half of the students received a short-term suspension. These results would compare favorably with those obtained from a zero tolerance approach, in which a large number of students might be expelled or receive long-term suspensions from school.

Third, the principals reported relatively few cases in which the student's behavior worsened or the student's relationship with the threat recipient worsened. However, it would be important to assess threat outcomes in more depth. Students involved in these cases were not contacted to obtain their perspective or to assess how well they were faring in their academic and social adjustment. Data on the outcomes for the threat recipients would be useful in assessing how the threat affected them and whether they regarded the conflict or problem as resolved. There are multiple avenues for further study in this area.

More research on threat outcomes. A related area for future study is the investigation of reported versus unreported student threats. It seems important to learn how students respond to threats, how they determine that a threat is serious, and what factors influence their decision to seek help. Studies of bullying indicate that a large proportion of students do not seek help from adults when they are bullied, although most students do seek help if the bullying persists (Unnever & Cornell, 2003, 2004). Evidently, most students do not seek help in response to student threats, perhaps because they do not regard the threat as serious or they feel that they can resolve the situation without adult assistance.

More insight is needed into various means of resolving threats that do come to the attention of school authorities. What methods (e.g.,

mediation, individual counseling, disciplinary consequences) are most effective for different kinds of threats? Schools have an obligation to respond to reported threats, so a "no response" comparison is not possible. However, it would be useful to compare threat-resolution strategies, recognizing that the critical outcome variables should go beyond whether the threat is carried out, because violent outcomes should be very low in all circumstances. It would be particularly useful to study emotional, social, and academic outcomes for the students who made threats as well as for threat recipients. Finally, it is important to study disciplinary outcomes to determine whether threat assessment can reduce the disproportionality observed across ethnic and gender groups and for students receiving special education services (Skiba, 2002; Skiba et al., 2000).

More research on implementing threat assessment. It is critical to identify the key systems variables that contribute to the successful implementation of a threat assessment program. Future trials can determine how easily our findings generalize to other schools. We recognize that threat assessment procedures may need adaptation and adjustment in different school environments. Although the two school divisions studied have substantial numbers of students with serious behavioral and emotional problems, as well as students living in disadvantaged conditions, a natural question is how threat assessment can be applied in a school with even greater challenges or more limited staff resources.

These observations lead to the hypothesis that three factors are relevant to the successful implementation of threat assessment. First, it is important for the team to have a common body of information about the nature and scope of school violence—and a shared conceptual framework concerning student threats—so as to resist fears of school shootings that provoke extreme responses. The training program begins by disputing public perceptions that schools are dangerous places, and it presents statistical findings that school safety has improved over the past 10 years.

Second, a multidisciplinary team-oriented approach is helpful for a variety of reasons, including the greater expertise and resources that can be brought to bear on a problem and the increased confidence of decision makers (e.g., school administrators) that they are taking a safe and appropriate course of action.

Third, the administrative leadership in the superintendent's office of each school division should be credited for supporting the implementation of a divisionwide approach. School principals have numerous competing demands and cannot devote equal attention to all issues and concerns. Threat assessment must be recognized as an important and worthwhile endeavor for it to be successfully implemented and practiced. The principal is instrumental in engaging the school staff and making threat assessment an accepted part of school policy.

Threat assessment is not intended as a stand-alone approach but rather a component of a comprehensive school violence prevention effort (Osher et al., 2004; Sprague et al., 2001). Threat assessment is not a substitute for other violence prevention efforts but rather a means of investigation that leads directly to targeted interventions; such interventions deal with conflicts and emerging problems before they result in violence. Threat assessment can be especially useful in helping schools to use resources in an efficient manner, because it offers schools a way to focus on threatening situations and to make reasoned judgments in distinguishing those situations that require more intensive intervention from those that can be more easily resolved.

CHAPTER 9

SCHOOLWIDE VIOLENCE PREVENTION

Threat assessment should be regarded as one component of a comprehensive school safety plan (Osher et al., 2004; Trump, 1998, 2000). A comprehensive plan contains three levels of intervention that can be represented as a pyramid of services (see *Figure 16*) (Dwyer & Osher, 2000; Sprague & Walker, 2000). At the base of the pyramid are schoolwide programs that serve all students by helping to maintain a disciplined, caring, and supportive environment. At the middle level are programs for students identified as being at risk for behavioral difficulties, and at the top level are services for a small group of students who require individualized interventions. This trichotomy corresponds to the universal, selective, and targeted interventions described by Sprague and Walker (2000). This chapter will focus on universal and selective services at the bottom and middle levels, respectively; the next chapter will describe individualized or targeted services at the top level. The pyramid describes a model for threat prevention and intervention and is intended to be consistent with more general

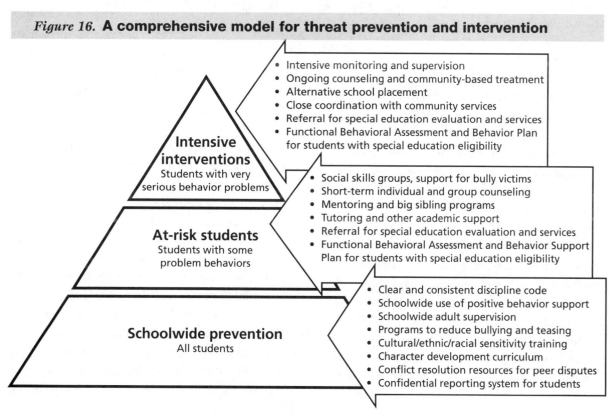

Figure 16. **A comprehensive model for threat prevention and intervention**

Intensive interventions
Students with very serious behavior problems

- Intensive monitoring and supervision
- Ongoing counseling and community-based treatment
- Alternative school placement
- Close coordination with community services
- Referral for special education evaluation and services
- Functional Behavioral Assessment and Behavior Plan for students with special education eligibility

At-risk students
Students with some problem behaviors

- Social skills groups, support for bully victims
- Short-term individual and group counseling
- Mentoring and big sibling programs
- Tutoring and other academic support
- Referral for special education evaluation and services
- Functional Behavioral Assessment and Behavior Support Plan for students with special education eligibility

Schoolwide prevention
All students

- Clear and consistent discipline code
- Schoolwide use of positive behavior support
- Schoolwide adult supervision
- Programs to reduce bullying and teasing
- Cultural/ethnic/racial sensitivity training
- Character development curriculum
- Conflict resolution resources for peer disputes
- Confidential reporting system for students

intervention models (Dwyer & Osher, 2000; Sprague & Walker, 2000).

The foundation for a safe school rests on creating a caring community where students feel safe and secure. Safety and security are based on two conditions: (1) an orderly, predictable environment where school staff provide appropriate supervision and discipline; and (2) a school climate where students feel connected to the school and supported by their teachers and other school staff. These conditions require an organized, schoolwide approach that involves all school staff. Positive Behavior Support is an approach that offers practical advice on achieving these conditions (Mayer, 1995; Metzler, Biglan, Rusby, & Sprague, 2001; Sprague & Golly, 2004; Sprague, Sugai, & Walker, 1998; Sugai & Horner, 1994).

POSITIVE BEHAVIORAL APPROACHES TO DISCIPLINE

As used in this manual, Positive Behavior Support (PBS) refers to a family of approaches that emphasizes positive behavioral interventions and systems change to construct a stable, predictable, and supportive environment for students (Mayer, 1995; Sugai et al., 2000). PBS stresses that students should be taught social and communication skills so that they can engage in civil and respectful behavior without resorting to aggressive, disruptive, or disobedient actions.

A safe and orderly school begins with clear rules and consistent discipline. Schools should have simple, straightforward rules for student behavior that are disseminated to every student and parent. Students should be expected to learn the rules and understand their purpose. School staff should reinforce, model, and enforce compliance with the rules in a consistent, constructive manner (Metzler et al., 2001; Sprague & Golly, 2004).

One of the recommended rules is, "Treat others with respect." This rule means that students (and adults, too) are not permitted to make disrespectful remarks, including teasing, insulting, bullying, and threatening others. The "respect rule" can be supported by curriculum units that teach effective ways to express criticism and disagreement without being disrespectful. In addition, an important aspect of the PBS program is that, when students break a rule, the consequences should include an opportunity to engage in appropriate behavior that corrects the mistake. For example, a student who makes an insulting remark is required to apologize and come up with an alternative way to express his or her opinion that is not disrespectful.

Positive discipline begins with explaining to a student why his or her behavior violated a school rule and what behavior would have been appropriate. Next, the student may experience a consequence for this behavior, such as a temporary loss of privileges that are naturally linked to the behavior. For example, a student who misbehaves during recess should have a suspension of recess privileges. Consequences should be calibrated to the seriousness of the misbehavior. This approach is contrary to the zero tolerance approach in which all infractions result in the same harsh consequences—such as expelling a student for a minor violation—regardless of the situation or context.

It is important that there be clear, immediate consequences for misbehavior and that all staff enforce these consequences in a fair, consistent, and dependable manner. Students must come to expect that they will receive consequences for their behavior and that those consequences are not dependent on which school staff member happens to be nearby. Student discipline must be recognized and appreciated by students as "firm, but fair" (Sprague & Golly, 2004). They must have a sense that the consequences were fairly applied to them and that other students would have received the same consequences for identical behavior. Otherwise, students fail to experience the consequence as a response to their behavior

> A safe school begins with clear discipline policies and simple rules that all students can understand. One rule we recommend is, "Treat others with respect." Teach students that threats of violence are violations of this rule.

and instead interpret it as a personal attack or act of rejection.

The one exception to the principle of identical consequences for identical behavior is that consequences should escalate for repeated misbehavior. The student who is late for class repeatedly should receive a more stringent consequence than the student who is late for the first time. School staff should explain to students that consequences escalate with repeated misbehavior, and students should always be informed when they are receiving consequences for repeated misbehavior rather than for a single incident.

In addition to consequences for misbehavior, a PBS approach makes use of incentives and rewards for appropriate behavior. There should be schoolwide policies and practices that recognize and reward good behavior (Metzler et al., 2001). Teachers should emphasize positive consequences for behavior that is compliant with the rules. Positive consequences can range from routine verbal praise to rewards for extended periods of good behavior.

REASONS STUDENTS DON'T REPORT THREATS

- "I didn't know who to tell."
- "I didn't think he [or she] would really do it."
- "I didn't want to get him [or her] in trouble."
- "I didn't want to be a *snitch*."

Every teacher should make sure that all students understand the importance of reporting threats. The most important points to emphasize with students are:

- Students can go to *any* teacher or staff member to report a threat.
- Students should report *any* threat that is not clearly a joke.
- A classmate will be in *more* trouble if a threat is carried out than if it is prevented.
- *Seeking help* to prevent someone from being hurt is not snitching.

HOW CAN THREATS BE IDENTIFIED?

Even in the best functioning school, there will be occasional incidents that result in student threats. For this reason, school staff should be prepared to identify threats and alert the threat assessment team.

Threat assessment is heavily dependent on student willingness to report threats to school staff. The FBI study of school shootings (O'Toole, 2000) found that many potential shootings were prevented because students reported threats made by their classmates. Unfortunately, in many of the school shootings that did occur, students failed to report threats made by their classmates. It is instructive to consider the reasons students give for not reporting threats. Often students do not report threats because they are uncertain whom to contact, they are unsure if the threat will be carried out, and, most of all, they do not want to be regarded as a snitch who caused someone to be in trouble. Teachers should spend time with each class explaining the difference between snitching on someone and seeking help to prevent someone from being hurt. Students should understand that all school staff are available to listen to their concerns and that they should be willing to come forward anytime there is reason to think someone *might* be in danger of being harmed. This information should be presented to students at the beginning of each school year and reemphasized as necessary.

HOW CAN THREATS BE PREVENTED?

In order to prevent threats, it is useful to consider how they originate. Threats are often the product of an unresolved conflict or dispute between students or, occasionally, between students and school staff. The frequency of such threats could be reduced if all students were routinely taught how to resolve conflicts and disputes. When inevitably there are some conflicts that students cannot resolve, there should be resources available to help them, such as counselors trained in conflict resolution or, for some situations, peer mediators.

Another common source of student threats is bullying. Bullies use threats to intimidate and dominate their victims. Conversely, victims of bullying may use threats as a way to retaliate. For example, a student who has been teased by a group of students may threaten to commit an act of violence. In either situation, the incidence of threats could be reduced if a school had an effective program to prevent bullying.

DO VIOLENCE PREVENTION EFFORTS WORK?

For many years there was a pervasive belief that "nothing works" in preventing juvenile delinquency and violence. In part, this belief reflected the lack of research evidence supporting the effectiveness of various delinquency prevention programs. However, there is now solid evidence that school violence can be prevented or reduced with well-conceived and carefully implemented interventions. Wilson, Lipsey, and Derzon (2003) conducted a meta-analysis of 221 studies of school-based interventions involving nearly 56,000 students. Each of these studies included pre- and post-assessment of at least one form of aggressive behavior, broadly defined to include fighting, bullying, assault, conduct disorder, and acting out. These researchers found a wide range in program effectiveness but calculated an average effect size of .25 for well-implemented demonstration programs. They estimated that an effect size of this magnitude would eliminate approximately half the incidents of fighting in a typical school year. Similarly, Wilson, Gottfredson, and Najaka (2001) found that school-based prevention programs reduced substance use, conduct problems, and truancy.

The most extensively studied programs are designed to enhance students' social competence (Wilson et al., 2003). A typical social competence program includes lesson plans for instructors to teach students how to resolve peer conflicts. Students are taught, often through role-playing and demonstration exercises, communication skills such as how to deflect criticism and assert their opinions in a nonprovocative manner. They

are taught how to listen and respond respectfully to others. They are presented with typical peer situations in which they must resolve a conflict or cope with disappointment. Some programs include a cognitive–behavioral component in which students learn relaxation techniques, practice self-monitoring, or rehearse step-by-step procedures for thinking through problems.

What are the characteristics of the most effective violence prevention programs? Not surprisingly, Wilson et al. (2003) found that quality of program implementation was critical. Schools that had difficulty fully implementing a program experienced less success, and programs that were implemented as part of a demonstration project—where presumably great attention was given to program fidelity—were more successful than programs operating under routine conditions. *Quality of program implementation cannot be stressed enough.* In their survey of 3,691 school-based prevention programs, Gottfredson and Gottfredson (2001) found that typical prevention efforts are not well integrated into normal school operations and that the school staff who implement these programs are in need of better training, support, and supervision.

Wilson et al. (2003) found that violence prevention programs were effective at all age levels and that there were no differences in program effectiveness associated with gender and ethnic composition of the samples. Both high-risk and low-risk students benefited from interventions, although, as might be expected, the degree of improvement was greater in high-risk populations, for whom there was greater room for change.

Programs delivered by teachers were most effective, followed by programs delivered by researchers, and then by those delivered by laypersons. Programs that delivered more intensive services and provided more one-on-one attention demonstrated stronger effects. An unexpected finding was that the demonstration programs that delivered academic services (such as tutoring and reading development) obtained the largest effect sizes. One intriguing hypothesis is that many students engage in aggressive behavior because of frustration over poor academic performance and that attention to their academic needs will pay dividends in good behavior.

WHAT KINDS OF PROGRAMS ARE AVAILABLE?

Fortunately, there are a multitude of effective violence prevention programs covering all grade levels and using a variety of intervention methods. An excellent summary can be found in *Safe, Supportive and Successful Schools: Step by Step* (Osher et al., 2004). Following is a sample of school-based programs that are particularly relevant to the prevention of student conflicts and aggressive behavior.

Elementary school programs. There are several well-designed and rigorously evaluated programs that teach social competence to elementary school children. One of the best-known programs, Interpersonal Cognitive Problem Solving (ICPS) (also known as "I Can Problem Solve") helps students to identify problems, recognize the feelings and perspectives of others, consider the consequences of alternative solutions, and then choose the best course of action. There are inexpensive manuals and workbooks—from preschool to grade 6—that can be used by either teachers or parents (Shure, 1992, 1996a, 1996b). Numerous evaluations, including multiyear follow-up studies, document that training improves student behavior and generalizes across classroom, home, and peer situations (Shure, 1997, 2001).

The Primary Mental Health Prevention (PMHP) project is one of the oldest and most respected school-based programs for identifying and treating preschool and early elementary school children at risk for emotional and behavioral problems (Cowen, Hightower, Pedro-Carroll, Work, & Wyman, 1996; Johnson, 2002). The basic PMHP model, which is used in more than 1,500 schools around the world, involves carefully supervised, paraprofessional counseling for students with emotional or behavioral problems. There are specialized components to teach social problem-solving, assist students with divorced parents, facilitate peer relationships, and encourage cooperative learning. A variety of large-scale, multiyear program evaluations involving thousands of students documented positive changes in the emotional and behavioral adjustment of PMHP students.

Promoting Alternative THinking Strategies (PATHS) is a comprehensive, developmentally based curriculum for teachers to use with elementary school children (Kusché & Greenberg, 1994). The goals of PATHS include teaching emotional literacy, improving social competence, alleviating and preventing emotional distress and behavioral problems, improving classroom atmosphere, and enhancing student–teacher relationships (Kusché, 2002). A two-year follow-up study of 18 special education classrooms found a reduction in teacher-reported internalizing and externalizing behaviors (Kam, Greenberg, & Kusché, 2004).

Second Step Violence Prevention (available: http://www.cfchildren.org/ssf/ssf/ssindex) teaches anger management, empathy, and impulse control to students in grades 1–3. Studies found that Second Step increases prosocial behaviors and reduces antisocial behaviors (Grossman et al., 1997; Taub, 2002). One study found that the integration of Second Step with positive behavioral support was especially effective (Sprague et al., 2001). A survey of California school counselors ranked Second Step first among violence prevention programs (Oppitz, 2003).

Middle and high school programs. Aggression Replacement Training (ART) (Goldstein, Glick, Reiner, Zimmerman, & Coultry, 1987) (available: http://www.aggressionreplacementtraining.org) was designed for middle and high school students, especially those with a history of aggressive behavior, and requires a highly skilled trainer. ART has three components: (1) "skillstreaming," to teach social behavior skills; (2) anger control, to recognize and avoid angry behavior; and (3) moral reasoning training, to enhance a sense of fairness, justice, and concern for others.

The Resolving Conflict Creatively Program (RCCP) (available: http://www.esrnational.org/es/rccp.htm) is one of the most widely used social competence programs and can be used from kindergarten through grade 12 (Lantieri, 2003). RCCP teaches students practical skills for resolving conflict and attempts to institutionalize a message of nonviolence throughout the school (Lantieri, DeJong, & Dutrey, 1996). RCCP's comprehensive program includes a classroom curriculum, a student-led mediation program, professional training and ongoing technical assistance for teachers, and training for parents and administrators.

Responding in Peaceful and Positive Ways (RIPP) is a sixth grade violence prevention program (Meyer, Farrell, Northup, Kung, & Plybon, 2000) (available: http://www.springeronline.com). A 25-session curriculum promotes nonviolent attitudes and the development of positive communication skills. RIPP also involves team-building activities, along with small group work, role playing, relaxation techniques, and repetition and rehearsal. Outcome studies indicate that the RIPP program lowers rates of fighting, bringing weapons to school, and in-school suspensions (Farrell, Meyer, & White, 2001; Farrell, Meyer, Sullivan, & Kung, 2003).

CAN WE PREVENT BULLYING?

After decades of neglect, bullying has become widely recognized as an important and pervasive problem in American schools (Espelage & Swearer, 2004; Sheras, 2002). A national study revealed that 30% of students (grades 6–10) reported moderate or frequent involvement in bullying as a bully or victim (Nansel et al., 2001). Studies of school shootings found that most of the perpetrators suffered from chronic teasing and harassment by their classmates and perceived themselves as victims (O'Toole, 2000; Vossekuil et al., 2002). At least 15 states have passed laws to address bullying (Limber & Small, 2003).

Unfortunately, bullying is so pervasive that it is sometimes regarded as a normal or inevitable part of growing up (Sheras, 2002). On the contrary, research indicates that school victimization has substantial and lasting effects on students' social and emotional adjustment (Boulton &

Underwood, 1992; Craig, 1998; Crick & Bigbee, 1998; Furlong, Chung, Bates, & Morrison, 1995; Gilmartin, 1987; Kochenderfer & Ladd, 1996; Neary & Joseph, 1994; Slee & Rigby, 1993). Repeatedly victimized students often experience a variety of mental health problems, including depression, anxiety, and low self-esteem. Victims tend to feel unsafe at school and are more likely than other students to have school attendance problems. Victims of chronic bullying continue to exhibit social adjustment problems in adulthood. Young bullies develop attitudes and values that lead to more serious aggressive behavior in adolescence. Adult tolerance for bullying sends the wrong message to students and promotes acceptance of coercion, harassment, derogation, and violence as means of controlling others.

There are many programs available to help schools undertake campaigns to reduce bullying (Garrity, Jens, Porter, Sager, & Short-Camilli, 1994; Griffin & Gross, 2004; Hoover & Oliver, 1996; Olweus, Limber, & Mihalic, 1999). It is not easy to stop bullying, and many studies have reported only small gains (Griffin & Gross, 2004; Smith, Schneider, Smith, & Ananiadou, 2004), but Olweus (1993) found a 50% reduction in bullying, as well as marked reductions in vandalism, truancy, and fighting.

SCHOOLWIDE BULLYING PREVENTION

1. Measure the prevalence of bullying.
2. Train staff to take an active role.
3. Establish clear school rules on bullying.
4. Educate parents about bullying.
5. Hold a schoolwide assembly.
6. Provide classroom instruction on bullying.
7. Identify students involved in bullying.
8. Measure progress in reducing bullying.

Schools should start by measuring the prevalence of bullying with a combination of student self-report and peer nomination measures (Cornell, Cole, & Sheras, in press). This information should be used for two purposes. First, information on the prevalence of bullying should be used to educate teachers and parents as to the importance of bullying as a schoolwide problem. Such information should motivate a schoolwide effort to revise policies and take action when bullying is identified. There should be schoolwide classroom instruction on the problem of bullying and how students should respond when they are recipients of bullying or observe their classmates being bullied.

Second, specific information from students naming perceived victims and bullies should be used by school administrators and counselors in follow-up interviews to confirm what kind of bullying, if any, is taking place. There should be individual interventions and disciplinary responses to students who engage in bullying. It also may be useful to provide individual or group counseling for victims of chronic bullying. In all cases, it is necessary to monitor and follow up to make sure that bullying does not continue and that students identified as bullies do not retaliate against their victims.

WILL THESE PROGRAMS WORK?

No strategy is effective for all youth or all settings. Every prevention program will have youth who fail, and, unfortunately, failure inevitably receives more attention than success and can distort perceptions of program effectiveness. Consider a counseling program that successfully teaches 99 students to resolve a conflict and avoid a fight but has 1 student who gets into a serious fight in the school lobby. Observers may judge the program by the single serious fight that occurred in a public place, unaware of the 99 successes. Prevention success is often invisible, whereas prevention failures are never overlooked.

One way to demonstrate that a program is effective is to collect baseline data showing the rate of violence or misbehavior prior to program implementation and then obtain follow-up data to document improvement. Research methodologists will, of course, point out the need for controlled conditions and comparison groups to obtain scientifically rigorous data, but for the practical purposes of documenting school improvement, an accurate monitoring system is sufficient. We stress that schools should make use of standardized surveys to measure student perceptions of school climate and safety (Furlong, Morrison, Skiba, & Cornell, 2004; Cornell et al., in press).

All programs are vulnerable to criticism if they fail to routinely document overall success rates. No program can be completely effective, and sometimes the expectations for prevention programs are too high. According to a scientific review of controlled studies, school-based violence prevention programs can reduce fighting in a school by about 50% (Wilson et al., 2003). This is a remarkable accomplishment that has been largely overlooked in the field of education. In medical fields, a treatment that improves outcomes by 10–15% is often considered a breakthrough, and, in law enforcement, a program that reduces crime by 10–15% would be regarded as effective.

Finally, even the best validated program will not succeed if it is not adequately funded and faithfully implemented by appropriately trained staff. More generally, programs must demonstrate adequate treatment fidelity; i.e., they must faithfully implement the actual treatment program as it was designed. All too often, programs have rushed to implement new treatment programs without adequate training and preparation, so that treatment failure is a result of poor implementation, not an inadequate treatment model (for example, see Henggeler, Melton, Brondino, Scherer, & Hanley, 1997).

The large number of intervention packages and programs available to schools might imply that it is simply a matter of selecting the one that seems most appealing or relevant to the school's needs. Programs are most likely to succeed if they are implemented by a committed school staff that is prepared to create a positive school environment for all students (Sprague & Golly, 2004; Sprague et al., 2001).

CHAPTER 10

INTERVENTIONS AFTER A STUDENT THREAT OF VIOLENCE

By Diana Browning Wright and Dewey Cornell

Threat assessment is a process that goes beyond assessment to include interventions to address the issues underlying the student's threat. Once the threat assessment team has taken the immediate steps to protect potential victims, planning must turn to constructing a follow-up plan to meet the student's educational and counseling needs and to monitor for the risk of violence. The purpose of this chapter is to describe the planning process for follow-up interventions after the immediate safety concerns have been addressed.

The ARMS process—Assessment, Referral, Monitoring, and Support—is a useful approach to developing an individualized behavior plan for students who have made threats of violence. If a student has special education status, the team must consider whether the student's threat represents a manifestation of his or her disability and what, if any, modifications to the student's IEP are needed. The ARMS approach will be illustrated with cases involving both general and special education students.

WHAT IS ARMS?

ARMS is a process that can be applied to any student behavior problem, but it was devised especially for those requiring a functional analysis of behavior (Nelson, Roberts, & Smith, 1998; O'Neill et al., 1997) leading to a Behavior Support Plan, as described in IDEA '97. The ARMS process

involves four activities, starting with *assessment* of the problem behavior, followed by *referral* of the student for needed services, *monitoring* of the student's response to the intervention, and *support* of the student's improved behavior (see *Figure 17*).

Figure 17. **Assess, refer, monitor, and support**

The assessment phase begins with the identification of the student's behavior as a threat. Team members have the task of determining the context and meaning of the threat, not only to judge the dangerousness of the threat, but also to assess what the student might need in order to resolve the underlying problem or conflict. A threat is often an indication that a student is in trouble, suffering from a problem he or she cannot resolve and using maladaptive or dysfunctional methods to cope. Assessment serves the purpose of identifying the student's intervention needs.

Once the team has assessed the student's needs, it can make referrals for appropriate services. A student with a serious mental disorder might be referred for psychiatric treatment, whereas another student might need substance abuse counseling. A student living in a stressful home might benefit from a referral for family therapy; in some cases, it may be necessary to seek social welfare services or to contact child protective services to report abuse or neglect. In addition to community-based services, the team may make referrals to school-based programs such as individual and group counseling, mediation services, mentoring, and academic support. And always the team must consider whether a student should be referred for special education services. If the student is already receiving such services, it is appropriate for the IEP team to reevaluate the special education plan. As described in the following paragraphs, the student's threatening behavior may be an indication that the plan is in need of amendment.

The team's responsibilities do not stop with making referrals. Someone on the team should be designated to monitor the student's participation in the recommended services. Especially if the student has made a substantive threat, it may be important to monitor services that were aimed at reducing the risk of violence. Monitoring could range from checking with community agencies to obtaining formal reports of treatment compliance. In-school monitoring could include having a team member communicate regularly with teachers, having the student meet weekly with a counselor, or in some other way making sure that an intervention plan is working. For example, if a student has made threats in the form of bullying his or her classmates, then it makes sense to speak with the classmates to make sure the bullying has ceased.

Finally, the team may develop a Behavior Support Plan that attempts to teach adaptive behaviors that replace the maladaptive threatening behavior (Sprague & Golly, 2004). More generally, the Behavior Support Plan might help the student develop social and behavioral skills that divert him or her from a pathway leading to aggressive behavior. Behavior Support Plans often describe how teachers and other adults can interact with the student in a positive manner that models and reinforces appropriate behavior (Flannery, Sprague, & Todd, 1996; Sprague & Golly, 2004).

IDEA '97 described an intervention planning process based on functional assessment. A key assumption of functional assessment is that a student's behavior has a purpose or function in a particular context (Nelson, Roberts, & Smith, 1998; Skiba, Waldron, Bahamonde, & Michalek, 1998). The first task of a functional assessment is to determine the meaning or purpose of the student's behavior, which is consistent with the goals of a threat assessment. Under what circumstances does the student engage in the inappropriate behavior—in this case, a threat—and what contingencies or factors influence it? Once the context for the behavior has been adequately understood, it should be possible to identify a more appropriate behavior that can be taught to replace the undesirable behavior. The student's Behavior Support Plan is a set of instructions for school staff to follow in teaching the student how and when to replace the problem behavior with the desired appropriate behavior. For example, a student who is repeatedly provoking classmates with insulting and threatening remarks might be taught how to gain attention and respect from classmates by making more appropriate remarks.

A Behavior Support Plan usually operates on a micro-level and is not a substitute for a more comprehensive, macro-level intervention plan.

> IDEA '97 is the binding federal law at the time of publication of this manual, but procedures and requirements may change with the 2004 revision of IDEA and the accompanying new regulations. State laws and new court decisions also must be considered. Always check with your local special education department for current practices and requirements.

A Behavior Support Plan cannot accomplish the broader objectives of mental health treatment, but it can provide an important bridge between overall treatment goals and implementation of improved behavior in specific situations.

WHY ARE THERE SPECIAL PROVISIONS FOR STUDENTS WITH SPECIAL EDUCATION STATUS?

School authorities have a legal obligation to maintain a safe learning environment for all students, and therefore they are advised to establish and enforce a code of conduct (Jacob & Hartshorne, 2003). This code of conduct can provide for the removal of students who endanger others or disrupt the learning environment. Students with disabilities who engage in dangerous or disruptive behavior can be held to the same code of conduct and can be subject to the same disciplinary consequences as all other students, but, in these cases, school authorities have an additional responsibility to consider the relationship between the student's behavior and his or her disabling condition (Dwyer, 1997). Students should not, and legally cannot, be punished for disciplinary violations if the student's disability prevents him or her from understanding or complying with the school's code of conduct or rule. To make this point clear, Dwyer (1997) gives the compelling example of a student with Tourette's syndrome who repeats obscene words over and over but who obviously should not be punished for violating the discipline code prohibiting such language because his or her behavior is an involuntary product of a mental disorder.

Although it is easy to understand the rationale for excusing the involuntary verbal behavior of a student with Tourette's syndrome, most cases are less clear-cut. Oftentimes, a student with an emotional disturbance will engage in inappropriate behaviors—such as swearing and threatening—that seem to be voluntary and goal-directed responses to others. In these cases, the IEP team has the difficult task of determining whether the behavior is a manifestation of the student's disability.

A complicating factor is that the definition of ED recognizes a distinction between emotional disturbance and "social maladjustment" (IDEA, 1997, 34 CFR, § 300.7). Behaviors that are the product of social maladjustment alone do not qualify as emotional disturbance, although it is explicitly recognized in the law that a student could have both social maladjustment and emotional disturbance. In these cases where both factors are present, there is no clear guidance on determining whether the student's behavior is a manifestation of his or her disability, and there is the possibility that a student with a disability could engage in threatening behavior that is a product of social maladjustment and not his or her emotional disturbance. Such determinations depend heavily on the nature of the emotional disturbance, and, because the category of emotional disturbance is so heterogeneous, it is not possible to offer a general rule to resolve this thorny issue. IDEA '97 attempted to provide some (limited) guidance on the relationship between disability and behavior by raising two questions for consideration: (1) Did the student's disability impair his or her ability to understand the impact and outcome of the behavior; and (2) Did the disability impair the student's ability to control the behavior? It is hoped that this problematic issue will be addressed in the regulations for IDEA 2004.

Because there is no simple rule or standard to use in judging the relationship between disability and behavior in making a manifestation determination, each case must be judged on its own merits, taking into consideration all available information about the incident (Dwyer, 1997). A determination cannot be made based solely on the student's label or category of disability or on the student's general ability to "tell right from wrong." A manifestation determination also must include an analysis of the adequacy of the student's IEP and specifically whether the plan was both appropriate in design and properly implemented. If the IEP was not adequate, because it either did not address the identified problem or was not being properly implemented, the plan should be modified accordingly.

Disciplinary options. The 1997 revision of IDEA (34 CFR, § 300.121) offered several disciplinary options for students with disabilities who engage in dangerous behavior (Jacob & Hartshorne, 2003). A student with a disability may be suspended from school for disciplinary reasons following the same standards used for other students, but suspensions that cumulatively total more than 10 days in a single school year may be considered a change in placement. The IEP team must authorize any change in placement of a student with a disability.

In some cases, school authorities may want to remove the student from school for more than 10 days and place him or her in an alternative educational setting. IDEA '97 permitted such a placement for up to 45 calendar days, provided certain conditions are met (1997, 34 CFR, § 300.520). A 45-day placement is permitted if the student was found to have carried a weapon (or was involved in the possession, use, sale, or solicitation for sale of a controlled substance) at school or at a school function. In addition, a 45-day placement can be ordered by a hearing officer if the school is able to demonstrate, by a preponderance of the evidence, that (1) maintaining the student in his or her current placement is substantially likely to result in harm to self or others; (2) they have made reasonable efforts to minimize the risk of harm in the current placement; and (3) the proposed alternative is an appropriate setting and permits the student to continue to meet his or her IEP goals (Jacob & Hartshorne, 2003). IDEA 2004 may alter the duration and conditions of an alternative placement.

Still another option is for the IEP team to conduct a review of the student's current plan and consider the appropriateness of a change in placement. A change in placement may be made only if the IEP team determines that the change is necessary to provide a free, appropriate education in the least restrictive environment. In all cases, it is critically important to establish and maintain a supportive and collaborative relationship with the student's parents. The law permits much greater latitude when the parents agree with the plan.

The following case studies are intended to illustrate the development of intervention plans in response to student threats. The cases were managed under the provisions of IDEA '97. They are composites of actual cases, with fictional names and modified details to preserve anonymity. Additional case examples are available elsewhere (Cornell, 2004; Cornell & Williams, in press).

MITCH, THE DEPRESSED SIXTH GRADER

Around lunchtime, the assistant principal of Jefferson Middle School, Ms. Adams, received a telephone call from a sixth grade resource room teacher that a student named Mitch had threatened to shoot his classmates. Ms. Adams asked the teacher to escort the student to her office while a teaching assistant supervised the class. Ms. Adams briefly reviewed the facts of the incident with the teacher, who recounted that three students came to her and reported that Mitch had threatened to shoot them. Mitch had told them that he saw no reason for living and that he "might as well snuff myself and for that matter all of you with my dad's gun. I know where it is!" When the teacher confronted Mitch with the students' allegations, he responded, "So what?" and said nothing else.

Initial evaluation. Ms. Adams interviewed Mitch and found that he had little to say. He seemed sullen and angry and would not admit or deny threatening the other boys. At this point, it was evident to Ms. Adams that she could not readily resolve the incident as a transient threat, and therefore she had to regard it as a very serious substantive threat. She decided to contact the other members of the threat assessment team to begin collecting information about Mitch and the circumstances of the threat in order to decide what protective actions would be needed. She called Officer Monroe, and the two of them decided to start by interviewing the three boys who received the threat. The boys confirmed the threatening statement but could not explain why

Mitch had become angry at them. They reported that he had recently been "crabby a lot."

Mental health assessment. Ms. Adams also called upon the school psychologist, Mrs. Marbury, to conduct an emergency mental health assessment. Mitch's statement reflected both homicidal and suicidal intentions, and both demanded immediate investigation. Mrs. Marbury's primary task was to assess Mitch's mental state and whether he had a plan to harm himself or others. Mitch reported feeling sad and hopeless. He related that his parents had been divorced for many years and that his father had died two months ago. He had had little contact with his father and did not know him very well, and he was now struggling with the idea that he would never know his father. Mitch was tearful and clearly distressed during the interview.

Mitch denied having access to a firearm. He could not identify any reasons for being angry at his friends except that he thought they were "always acting stupid" and he felt "left out all the time." He denied plans to harm himself but admitted that he felt like life was not worth living and he might be better off dead. He agreed that he was not going to hurt himself. Mrs. Marbury concluded that Mitch had symptoms of depression and suicidal thoughts that warranted concern and that he should be referred for treatment. Mrs. Marbury wanted to get additional information before completing her assessment, but, based on her initial interview, it did not appear that Mitch had plans to shoot anyone, and he seemed to have made the statement out of anger and frustration.

Parent contact. The principal contacted Mitch's mother, Mrs. Randolph, and informed her of the incident. She explained that Mitch would be suspended from school for five days, and during this time they would complete a safety evaluation and develop a plan for meeting Mitch's educational needs. The principal encouraged Mrs. Randolph to participate in this evaluation. When Mrs. Randolph came to school, she met with Officer Monroe and Ms. Adams. Mrs. Randolph assured Officer Monroe that Mitch did not have access to a firearm at home. Officer Monroe explained

the seriousness of the situation but indicated that he was not going to arrest Mitch or press charges against him. Mrs. Randolph signed a release form for Mrs. Marbury to complete her evaluation and set up an appointment for herself and her son to meet with Mrs. Marbury the following day. Mrs. Marbury advised Mrs. Randolph that Mitch seemed depressed and suicidal and that he should be closely supervised. She recommended that they seek further evaluation and treatment, and she provided them with contact information for local mental health professionals.

Notification of victims' parents. The next task for the school principal was to contact the parents of the three boys who had been threatened. She described to them what she knew about the threat incident and the steps they had taken to investigate it. She disclosed to them the name of the boy who made the threat and explained that he had been suspended from school until a decision could be made about his return to school. Mrs. Adams promised to keep them informed and emphasized the importance of working with them to resolve the situation. Officer Monroe also contacted the parents to assure them that he had investigated the threat and would continue to monitor the situation.

Safety evaluation. The school counselor, Mrs. Jay, reviewed Mitch's records and spoke with his teachers, and the next day she presented a summary to other team members. Mitch had received special education services in a resource program since second grade for a mild learning disability affecting written language. He also exhibited some problems with attention, but not hyperactivity. He had a GPA of 2.8 and was generally well behaved in the classroom and well regarded by his teachers. Mitch did not have a history of aggressive or threatening behavior. His science teacher observed that earlier in the day he had reprimanded Mitch for failing to turn in a homework assignment.

The principal decided that there was no reason to pursue expulsion or a change in school placement for disciplinary reasons, and, because a five-day suspension did not constitute a change in school placement, there was no need for the IEP team to make a manifestation determination or conduct a formal Functional Behavioral Assessment. However, the team did recommend that the IEP team develop a Behavior Support Plan to monitor future behaviors and codify school-based support for Mitch through this difficult time. (See Mitch Randolph's Behavior Support Plan in the Appendix.) The threat assessment team consensus was that Mitch was not a safety threat to others and had no plan to harm others, but that his threat was more the act of a despondent student making a plea for help.

Mitch's mother agreed to take her son to a private therapist to address his grief issues and suicidal thinking. She was an active participant in planning support for Mitch but declined the offer of in-school counseling because she preferred to use a therapist from the family's faith community. She agreed that Mitch would attend a conflict mediation session with the three boys before returning to school (with consent from the parents of the three boys). She agreed that Mitch could have regular contact with the counselor to monitor his grades and his relationship with his peers and that the counselor would contact her if there was any indication of further problems. Finally, Mrs. Randolph signed a release of information permitting the school principal to speak with the parents of the three boys and explain to them the circumstances under which Mitch would be returning to school.

RAMON, THE GANG MEMBER

Mr. Jackson, the assistant principal of Northridge High School, received a telephone call Thursday morning from a distressed mother of a ninth grade student named Kirk Gibbs. Kirk was afraid to come to school because a classmate named Ramon had threatened to kill him. Mrs. Gibbs demanded that the school "do something about this boy who has threatened my son." Mr. Jackson knew Ramon well, because he had been referred to the office numerous times for disciplinary violations such as refusing to cooperate in class, swearing at teachers, and physical fighting. Mr. Jackson

invited Mrs. Gibbs to bring Kirk to his office so that they could go over exactly what happened.

Initial evaluation. Mrs. Gibbs brought Kirk to school later than morning. With great reluctance, Kirk reported that he had an argument with Ramon during PE class last week. The two continued exchanging words throughout the week, until the preceding day, when Ramon told Kirk, "I'll have my homeboys kill you." Kirk believed Ramon to be a new member of a gang and was concerned that the other gang members would come after him. No other student had heard the threat, but several students had witnessed the arguments between Kirk and Ramon.

Mr. Jackson asked Kirk and his mother to speak with the school resource officer, Officer Ramirez. After Officer Ramirez heard the account, he advised Mr. Jackson that he already had some information about the incident. He had heard about the conflict between Kirk and Ramon from other students. These students had observed the arguments between them but had either not witnessed or not reported the alleged threat. Officer Ramirez knew that Ramon lived in a neighborhood with an active gang, and it had been reported to him that Ramon and another boy had recently joined the gang.

Mr. Jackson interviewed Ramon but found him to be uncooperative. Ramon refused to admit that he knew Kirk, saying, "I don't know the punk." He denied threatening Kirk and, when asked if he had joined a gang, would not respond. Mr. Jackson decided that Kirk's report of being threatened was credible and that it constituted a very serious substantive threat.

Parent contact. Mr. Jackson left Ramon under the supervision of Officer Ramirez while he called Ramon's parents. Both parents were immigrants with limited knowledge of English. Ramon's mother, Mrs. Santiago, came to the school accompanied by a relative who could help translate. Mr. Jackson informed Mrs. Santiago that her son was being suspended from school because of his threat against another student. Mrs. Santiago indicated through the translator that she did not believe her son was a gang member and that she would not permit him to be a gang member. Mr. Jackson then invited Ramon and Officer Ramirez to join the interview. Ramon again denied making the threat, but, when Officer Ramirez stated his belief that Ramon had recently joined a gang, Ramon exclaimed, "Who told you that?" Mr. Jackson and Officer Ramirez expressed their concern to Mrs. Santiago that she keep Ramon under close supervision.

Mental health assessment. The school psychologist, Mrs. Robinson, met briefly with Ramon, but he was unwilling to speak with her. She invited Ramon to meet with her again in two days. Mrs. Robinson knew Ramon because he received special education services for a learning disability and she had conducted a triennial reevaluation the previous spring. When he did meet with her two days later, Ramon participated in the interview but declined to say anything about being in a gang or threatening Kirk. No indications of serious emotional disturbance or new mental health concerns were uncovered. The psychologist believed that Ramon was highly invested in impressing his peers and tended to engage in disruptive, attention-seeking behavior that he believed would increase his status. He also seemed susceptible to the influence of older boys, and this would include likely gang members.

Safety evaluation. The threat assessment team had serious concerns about Ramon because of his history of disciplinary violations and the news that he had recently joined a gang. Because he was unwilling to cooperate or even admit knowing Kirk, it was not possible to determine his intentions or assess whether the conflict between them might be resolved. In addition, Kirk was now frightened that other gang members might come after him. In the course of its investigation, the team learned that Ramon had been before the juvenile court for an assault that took place in his neighborhood and that he was on probation. The probation officer was contacted and agreed to participate as a team consultant.

The team decided that it would be safer for all parties if Ramon were transferred to an alternative school and separated as much as possible from gang members. Accordingly, Ramon was placed in an interim alternative placement for 45 calendar days. During this time, his current IEP goals could be met while the IEP team met to consider a revision to his educational plan. Mrs. Santiago agreed to the change in placement, having become concerned over Ramon's increasing anger and rebelliousness at home and now suspecting that he might indeed have joined a neighborhood gang.

The IEP team met to review Ramon's plan. His plan seemed adequate for meeting his academic needs as a student with a learning disability, but there had been no Behavior Support Plan for addressing his anger and uncooperativeness. The principal wanted to recommend Ramon for expulsion because of his repeated disciplinary violations. The principal felt it was important to crack down on gang members by removing them from school. The IEP team held the required manifestation review meeting to determine if Ramon's discipline violations were a manifestation of his disability. The IEP team determined that Ramon's recent threat was an extension of previous milder threats and aggressive behavior at school that should have been addressed, but had not been included, in his current plan. Therefore, they concluded that no "supplementary aids and supports" for his increasing behavior problems had been provided and, therefore, at the time of the behavior, the IEP in place was inadequate. If an IEP is judged to be inadequate for this reason, then the student cannot receive a disciplinary change in placement or expulsion.

Although Ramon could not be expelled from school for disciplinary purposes due to an inadequate IEP at the time of the behavior, there were still several options for ensuring school safety: (1) The school district could request a change in placement to provide supports that would be available only in the other setting (if the parents disagreed with this request, the issue would be resolved through normal IEP conflict resolution channels); (2) the school district could request a hearing officer to order the student to continue being served in the interim alternative placement, based on a finding of dangerousness; (3) the school district could work with the juvenile court to determine if Ramon had violated his probation; or (4) the school district could seek a temporary restraining order to bar Ramon from attending school until placement issues were resolved.

A Functional Behavioral Assessment concluded that Ramon's behaviors were attempts to gain recognition and status from classmates and gang member peers. Therefore, the IEP team had the responsibility to develop a Behavior Support Plan to deal with this problem.

The threat team leader concluded, with team agreement, that Ramon posed a threat to others if he remained at school and that it would be difficult to keep him from associating with gang members. The probation officer concurred and indicated that Ramon could face the prospect of violating his probation status and being committed to a juvenile correctional facility. Ramon's parents did not want their son to be sent to a juvenile correctional facility, and they wanted help in separating him from gang influences, so they were willing to consider an alternative placement. The IEP team recommended that Ramon could be placed in a sheltered setting designed to help juveniles separate from gangs. Ramon's parents accepted this recommendation. A sample Behavior Support Plan for Ramon is in the Appendix.

CARLIE, A VICTIM OF SOCIAL BULLYING

Carlie, a 15-year-old high school sophomore of Korean descent, was brought to the principal's office by the school resource officer. Carlie's teacher summoned the school resource officer after observing her threaten another girl named Brittany with a pair of scissors. Carlie pointed the scissors toward Brittany and exclaimed, "Maybe you should be dead!" The look on Carlie's face and the tone of her voice were clearly threatening to Brittany, who jumped back in obvious fear. The teacher ordered Carlie to put the scissors down and she complied. Then the teacher called the school resource officer, who came immediately to the classroom. By this time Carlie was sitting at her desk with her head down.

Initial evaluation. The principal, Mrs. Behrens, asked Carlie what had happened in the classroom and why she had done what she did. Carlie was tearful and begged the principal not to tell her parents. The principal knew that Carlie and her family had immigrated to the United States about 10 years ago and was aware that Korean parents are often very strict about proper behavior at school. Carlie said she was sorry and that she had never done anything like that before, but she had just felt so angry at Brittany for laughing at her that she had acted without thinking. She insisted she would never hurt anyone, but she just couldn't stand the other girls laughing at her all the time. They knew it hurt her feelings, and they just kept doing it every day, always finding something wrong with how she dressed or how she talked. Several of the comments contained ethnic slurs and references to Carlie's immigrant status. This morning the girls had giggled at a pair of shoes Carlie was wearing, which were old and dirty. Brittany had just looked disapprovingly at the shoes and commented, "Those shoes look really dead, you know." Carlie then picked up the scissors from a table and made the threatening statement, "Maybe you should be dead."

Mrs. Behrens next interviewed Brittany, who admitted that Carlie's threat followed her remark about Carlie's shoes. Brittany was quick to point out, "Maybe I shouldn't have laughed at her shoes, but there's no way she's justified in coming after me with those scissors." The principal agreed. Brittany said that she was truly frightened at Carlie's sudden action, because she had never known Carlie to show such anger. She said she did not think Carlie was going to attempt to hurt her but she would like to know what Carlie was thinking now. The principal knew Brittany was one of the more popular girls in the tenth grade and was part of a group of girls who were known to make fun of other girls. In middle school, Carlie had been friends with several of these girls, but in high school their friendships had waned, and now the girls actively snubbed Carlie and excluded her from their activities. Carlie had no history of discipline problems at school and made good grades, but she had no close friends.

Mrs. Behrens asked each girl if they would be willing to meet and talk about the incident. The two girls met with a school social worker who was trained in conflict mediation (while the principal was called away on another matter), and each presented her perspective on what had happened. Carlie apologized to Brittany for threatening her and promised she would never hurt her. Brittany accepted Carlie's apology and said she had not realized how upset Carlie was over the teasing she received about her clothing and speech. The school social worker recognized there was a theme of ethnic prejudice in several of the incidents that Carlie recounted and that these incidents involved a group of girls. She decided to follow up on this issue once the immediate incident was addressed.

The principal carefully considered what to do about the incident, recognizing that threat assessment and disciplinary consequences are distinguishable processes. The principal first considered the issue of threat assessment, because she had to consider whether to take further protective action in order to maintain the safety of Brittany and other students. After discussing the matter with several team members, the principal decided Carlie's threat was transient, for several reasons. The threat was evidently expressed in anger and without prior planning. Carlie did not have a history of violence, and there was no evidence that she intended to carry out the threat. On the contrary, she retracted the threat and made what seemed to be a sincere apology, and the apology was accepted and reciprocated by Brittany. There did not seem to be grounds for considering the threat to be substantive and for taking protective action to prevent Carlie from harming someone.

From a disciplinary perspective, Carlie had engaged in a disruptive, aggressive act, and her use of scissors made her behavior particularly serious. In some cases, a threat using a weapon could be grounds for a long-term suspension or even expulsion from school. However, in light of circumstances of this case and Carlie's previous good record, the principal decided that a short-term suspension would be appropriate.

The policy at this school was to give a five-day suspension to students who engaged in a physical fight, and, although there was no physical contact in this case, the principal decided that a five-day suspension was warranted because of Carlie's use of scissors to threaten Brittany.

The school resource officer advised the principal that Carlie's behavior could be considered an assault with a deadly weapon and that conceivably he could arrest her and place her in a juvenile detention facility. However, he said that in light of her record of good behavior and the circumstances of the incident, he did not think it was necessary to arrest her. He also could initiate charges in the juvenile court without arresting her, but in a situation like this he preferred to rely on the school discipline process. He pointed out that he would speak with Brittany's parents and that they would have the right to initiate charges even if he chose not to do so.

Follow-up. The school social worker held several meetings with Brittany and her friends, discussing with them the nature of their interactions with other girls. The counselor introduced them to the concept of "social bullying" and talked with them about the stress of being in high school and striving to be popular and accepted. She also addressed the subject of ethnic and racial bias. As a result of these meetings, the counselor proposed to the principal that the high school address the topic of social bullying in ninth grade health classes. As part of the school's annual "Citizenship Week," the principal invited a speaker to lead a school assembly on the status of immigrants and the special problems they face in coming to the United States. The principal also emphasized to teachers the need to be more aware of the problems faced by their immigrant students and to seek out opportunities to identify and respond to their needs.

Carlie met with the school social worker weekly for the remainder of the term. Their sessions addressed Carlie's anxiety over how students would perceive her after the scissors incident, her shyness and insecurity about making friends, and her fears of disappointing her parents if she did not make high grades. A sample Behavior Support Plan for Carlie is in the Appendix.

CONCLUSION

Threat assessment involves more than just assessing the student's threat. Threat assessment involves an assessment of the underlying problem that generated the threat and the development of an intervention plan that will address that problem, thereby reducing the risk of violence. The ARMS acronym helps team members remember that assessment is the first stage in a process that also includes referring the student for services, monitoring the student's response to services, and supporting the student by designing Behavior Support Plans. In cases of students with special education eligibility, the threat assessment team must work closely with the IEP team.

CHAPTER 11

IMPLEMENTING THREAT ASSESSMENT

HOW CAN THREAT ASSESSMENT BE IMPLEMENTED AT MY SCHOOL?

In order to implement threat assessment, there should be formal approval and support from the central administration of the school division. Ideally, threat assessment should be implemented on a divisionwide basis, with divisionwide training and uniform policies at each school. Implementation should begin with the superintendent's office and school board, which must understand and support the change in order for it to be successful.

It is understandably difficult for schools to make systematic changes and for school personnel to assume new roles and responsibilities at a time when there is great pressure to meet new federal and state requirements to improve student achievement and respond to other provisions of the No Child Left Behind Act of 2001 (2002). Nevertheless, threat assessment should be regarded as part of a comprehensive effort to maintain school safety, and this effort serves the larger purpose of creating an environment that is conducive to learning. Threat assessment should not be regarded as an additional burden for school staff but rather a means of maintaining a safe environment in which learning and achievement can take place.

Properly implemented, threat assessment should save time and facilitate the work of school administrations and student support services. Successfully resolving a threat and preventing a violent act are certainly more cost-effective than dealing with the aftermath of a violent incident. Moreover, by using threat assessment to quickly resolve transient threats and take prompt action in

> Threat assessment should not be burdensome to school staff, because it is a means of increasing efficiency by quickly resolving transient cases and targeting resources to the most serious cases. Preventing a violent act is always more efficient than dealing with the aftermath.

response to substantive threats, school personnel can work more efficiently and focus resources for student support and intervention where they are needed most.

WHAT POLICIES MUST BE CHANGED?

Threat assessment does not require major changes in school discipline policy for most school divisions. School principals retain a wide degree of latitude in determining disciplinary consequences, and, if anything, threat assessment gives principals a basis for even greater latitude, because they are guided to consider the meaning and context of the student's behavior.

A threat assessment team must consider the legal rights and special learning needs of students who have special education eligibility, but this is not a change from existing discipline policies. Threat assessment can be conducted in a manner that is consistent with all provisions of IDEA '97, although it is usually necessary to review and, in some cases, revise the student's IEP. School administrators are advised to remain up to date on federal and state laws and regulations that govern general and special education services.

WHAT WRITTEN POLICIES SHOULD BE IN PLACE?

Most schools have written documentation of discipline practices or a student code of conduct. Below and continuing on the following page is a list of provisions that school administrators should consider including in their student code of conduct or in other documentation of their practices.

WHAT ARE THE STEPS INVOLVED IN IMPLEMENTING THREAT ASSESSMENT?

Each school must consider how to integrate threat assessment into its existing policies and practices and how to identify the personnel who are most qualified and able to serve on threat assessment teams. These guidelines are truly guidelines and not a rigid prescription that must be followed in

---

MODEL POLICY FOR ADDRESSING STUDENT THREATS TO HARM OTHERS

Rationale: All students have the right to attend school in a safe and orderly environment that is conducive to learning. For this reason, there will be a standard procedure for investigating and responding to student threats to harm others.

Threat to harm others: A threat to harm others is defined as any spoken, written, or behavioral communication of intent to physically injure or harm someone else. A threat may be communicated directly to the intended victim or communicated to a third party.

Threat assessment: In order to maintain the safety of students and school personnel, student threats to harm others will be reported to the school principal. The principal or designee will lead a threat assessment team whose purpose is to conduct an assessment to determine the seriousness of the threat and take necessary steps to protect others and maintain a safe and orderly learning environment. The threat assessment team may include a representative from law enforcement, a school psychologist, a school counselor, and other members of the school staff designated by the principal.

Substantive and transient threats: A threat that is judged to involve sustained, serious intent to harm someone is termed a *substantive* threat. A threat that is judged not to be serious, because it can be immediately resolved so that there is no sustained intent to harm someone, is termed a *transient* threat. Judgments about the seriousness of a threat will be based on a consideration of its context and meaning. When the seriousness of a threat is unclear, the principal will treat the threat as substantive until its status is determined.

Disciplinary consequences: Both substantive and transient threats are subject to the full range of disciplinary consequences. In deciding on disciplinary consequences, the principal or designee will consider the seriousness of the threat and the degree to which the threat is disruptive to a safe and orderly environment conducive to learning for all students.

Continued on next page.

Parent notification: A threat assessment may include interviewing the student who was reported to make a threat and interviewing other students who have knowledge of the threat or information relevant to the safety of others. Parents will be notified promptly when a student has been interviewed about a reported threat.

Law enforcement notification: If a student is determined by the principal or designee to have made a substantive threat to harm others, and this threat involves a threat to kill, severely injure, or commit a sexual offense, the threat will be reported to law enforcement.

Notification of intended victims and their parents: If a student is determined by the principal or designee to have made a substantive threat to harm others, and the threat targets specific, identifiable victims, the intended victim(s) of the threat will be advised of the nature of the threat and the identity of the student who made the threat. If an intended victim is a student, the student's parent will also be notified.

Mental health assessment: If a student is determined by the principal or designee to have made a very serious substantive threat to harm others, the student may be seen by a school psychologist, counselor, clinical social worker, or other mental health professional to determine the student's immediate mental health status and safety needs.

Student suspension: When a student is determined to have made a substantive threat to harm others, the student may be suspended from school. During the suspension period, the threat assessment team will gather information necessary to develop a plan for meeting the student's educational needs and maintaining a safe and orderly school environment.

every respect. School divisions may need to adapt these recommendations for the staffing of threat assessment teams or to make slight modifications in procedures. (We welcome suggestions and feedback on improving these guidelines.) Very large school divisions may have different needs than smaller school divisions. Schools for students with special needs, especially alternative schools for students who have aggressive behavior problems, may need more resources and support options to deal with student threats than other schools. Threat assessment should be a cornerstone of an overall school security plan (Trump, 1998).

For all schools, a training process is recommended to prepare all school staff for the implementation of threat assessment procedures. Threat assessment team members require the most extensive training, but all school staff should be familiarized with the rationale and basic procedures for threat assessment. All school staff should be willing and able to identify and report threats and to cooperate with a threat investigation. After the staff have been trained, it is important to explain to students that threats are not acceptable behavior and that threats will receive disciplinary consequences. Students should be taught the difference between snitching on a peer and seeking help to prevent someone from being hurt, and they should be encouraged to report threats to a teacher or other school staff member. Every teacher and school staff member should let students know they are available to listen to their concerns. Parents and students should be informed that threats will be carefully investigated according to a standard procedure.

On the following pages are summaries that can be used as handouts or overheads in presenting information to school staff, parents, and students.

IMPLEMENTATION: STEP BY STEP

1. Obtain approval from the superintendent to adopt a threat assessment approach.

2. Revise the student code of conduct and discipline policies as needed.

3. Train the school administrators, law enforcement officers, and mental health professionals (counselors, psychologists, social workers, and others). Training should include a thorough review of the guidelines and team practice with mock cases.

4. Review the violence prevention and student support resources and programs available—in the school and in the community—that can be called upon in planning a response to individual student threats.

5. Hold inservice training to orient teachers and other school staff to threat assessment and clarify their role in reporting threats. See the staff handout.

6. Inform parents how the school will respond to student threats. (See the parent handout.)

7. Review school discipline policies with students and make clear that threats are not acceptable behavior. Explain the difference between "snitching" and seeking help and encourage students to seek help for threats. See the student handout.

8. Begin using threat assessment. Be sure to document all threats.

9. At the end of the year, review the threat assessment program and revise it as needed.

10. Each year, repeat the orientation for teachers, parents, and students.

STUDENT THREAT ASSESSMENT

Overview for school staff

This year, we will be using a standard procedure for responding to student threats of violence called "threat assessment." Threat assessment was recommended by the FBI and by the U.S. Secret Service and Department of Education in their studies of school violence. Threat assessment guidelines were developed and field-tested at the University of Virginia, and they have been adopted for use by hundreds of schools.

The basic idea is that, when a student communicates a threat to harm someone, the threat assessment team will determine how serious the threat is and what can be done to prevent the threat from being carried out. In most cases of school shootings, the student communicates a threat before taking action, and, if these threats can be identified, violence can be prevented. However, it is important not to treat all threats the same way, because most threatening statements made by students are not serious threats. The job of the threat assessment team is to determine how serious the threat is and how to respond to it. The team will investigate threats, quickly resolve the "transient" threats, and take further action to deal with the "substantive" threats. Research has shown that the vast majority of threats can be resolved safely and without drastic consequences such as school expulsion.

It is important to remember that it is highly unlikely that a student will carry out a threat to commit a homicide (national statistics show that the odds are no greater than 1 in 3 million that a student will be a victim of a homicide at school and that the average school can expect a student-perpetrated homicide only once every 12,800 years). In most cases, threats are a sign that a student is frustrated, angry, and needs help resolving a problem. A goal of threat assessment is to address this underlying problem.

If you know of a student who has made a threat, it is important to contact the school's threat assessment team.

What is a threat? A threat is any expression of an intent to harm someone. Threats may be spoken, written, or expressed in some other way, such as through gestures. Threats may be direct ("I am going to beat you up") or indirect ("Watch me beat him up after school"). A threat can be vague ("I'm going to hurt him") or implied ("You better watch out"). Possession of a weapon will be investigated as a possible threat.

What should I tell my students? Students are often reluctant to tell us about threats, because they don't want to be considered "snitches." We must teach students the difference between snitching and seeking help to prevent an act of violence. We must let students know we are always available to hear their concerns.

Who's on the team? See the attached information on team members.

STUDENT THREAT ASSESSMENT

Overview for parents

We use a standard procedure for responding to student threats of violence called "threat assessment." Threat assessment was recommended by the FBI and by the U.S. Secret Service and Department of Education in their studies of school violence. Threat assessment guidelines were developed and field-tested at the University of Virginia, and they have been adopted for use by hundreds of schools.

The basic idea is that when a student communicates a threat to harm someone, the threat assessment team will do an assessment to determine how serious the threat is and what can be done to prevent the threat from being carried out. In most cases of school shootings, the student communicates a threat before taking action, and, if these threats can be identified, violence can be prevented. However, it is important not to treat all threats the same way, because most threatening statements made by students are not serious threats. The job of the threat assessment team is to determine how serious the threat is and how to respond to it. The team will investigate threats, quickly resolve the "transient" threats, and take further action to deal with the "substantive" threats. Research has shown that the vast majority of threats can be resolved safely and without drastic consequences such as school expulsion.

It is important to remember that it is highly unlikely that a student will carry out a threat to commit a homicide (national statistics show that the odds are no greater than 1 in 3 million that a student will be victim of a homicide at school and that the average school can expect a student-perpetrated homicide only once every 12,800 years). In most cases, threats are a sign that a student is frustrated, angry, and in need of help resolving a problem. A goal of threat assessment is to address this underlying problem.

If your child knows about a student who has made a threat, it is important to contact the school principal.

What is a threat? A threat is any expression of an intent to harm someone. Threats may be spoken, written, or expressed in some other way, such as through gestures. Threats may be direct ("I am going to beat you up") or indirect ("Watch me beat him up after school"). A threat can be vague ("I'm going to hurt him") or implied ("You better watch out"). Possession of a weapon will be investigated as a possible threat.

What should parents do? Students are often reluctant to tell us about threats, because they don't want to be considered "snitches." Teach your son or daughter that there is a difference between snitching and seeking help to prevent an act of violence.

What if my child is involved in a threat? If your child makes a threat or is the target of a threat, we will contact you, advise you of our response, and seek your support and assistance in resolving the threat.

What Is a Threat?

A **threat** is when someone says he or she is going to hurt you or someone else.

Examples of threats:

o "I'm gonna bust you up."
o "I'm gonna get even with him."
o "Come watch what I'm gonna do to him."
o "I have a gun in my backpack."
o "I'm gonna blow this place up."

Sometimes students are just kidding when they make threats, but some threats are serious. Some threats are crimes. Don't make threats.

If you feel threatened or know about a serious threat to someone else, it is important to get help. ***Seeking help to prevent someone from getting hurt is not snitching.*** Let someone know there is a problem—tell a teacher, a counselor, or anyone on the school staff. We are here to help.

MAKE SURE YOU UNDERSTAND THE GUIDELINES

Team members should make sure they understand the guidelines before using them. In training workshops, teams review several hypothetical cases so that they can practice going through the steps of the decision tree. Teams should discuss recent cases or likely scenarios at their school in order to confirm that they have a common understanding of how they would proceed.

TEST YOURSELF

Team members can assess how well they understand the threat assessment guidelines by answering the questions in Test Your Knowledge of These Guidelines in the Appendix. For each question, assume you are the team leader asked to make a preliminary determination whether a threat has been made and, if so, what kind of threat it is. These examples do not include all of the information you would obtain for an actual case but are designed to test your knowledge of typical threat situations. Choose the most likely threat classification based on the limited information that you are provided. The correct answers to these cases are provided in the Appendix. Review these answers and be sure you understand them.

Now that the threat has been classified as transient, serious, or very serious, you have to decide the next step in your threat assessment. In some cases, there is more than one next step, so choose one or more of the options listed. In complex cases, there may be more steps to take than are listed, so just choose the best options among those that are offered. The answers are explained following the questionnaire.

Schools should undergo a group training experience and practice using the threat assessment guidelines. Training in student threat assessment can be accomplished with a five-hour workshop. The workshop should cover the following topics:

1. Nature and scope of youth violence, including misconceptions about school violence;

2. Rationale and purpose of threat assessment;

3. Explanation of the threat assessment guidelines and decision tree;

4. Legal and mental health issues in conducting student threat assessments; and

5. Case studies with team practice in simulated assessments.

For more information on training in these guidelines, see http://youthviolence.edschool. virginia.edu, contact youthvio@virginia.edu, or call 434-924-8929.

Threat Assessment Documentation 110

Behavior Support Plan 114

Behavior Support Plan—Case Examples 119

Test Your Knowledge of These Guidelines

      What Is the Most Likely Threat Classification? 131

      What Is the Most Likely Threat Classification?—Answers 134

      What Is the Next Step or Steps? 136

      What Is the Next Step or Steps?—Answers 140

Threat Assessment Documentation

This form should be used to document the threat assessment team's response to a student threat of violence. School administrators are advised to consult their division policy on record keeping for these forms.

General Information

Your name: _____ Position: _____ School: _____

Name of student _____

Date learned of threat: _____/_____/_____ Date threat occurred: _____/_____/_____

Type of threat: Transient   Serious Substantive   Very Serious Substantive

Who reported threat? _____ Location of Threat _____

_____

_____

What student said or did to express a threat (quote student if possible):

_____

_____

_____

Student Who Made Threat

Grade: _____

Gender: ☐ M ☐ F

Race:
☐ Caucasian ☐ African Am. ☐ Hispanic
☐ Asian Am. ☐ Other: _____

Special Education (if applicable):
☐ LD ☐ OHI ☐ MR
☐ ED ☐ Other: _____

Yes No—Had or sought accomplices

Yes No—Reported the threat as a specific plan

Yes No—Wrote plans or a list

Yes No—Repeated the threat over time

Yes No—Mentioned weapon in the threat

Yes No—Used weapon in the threat

Yes No—Had prior conflict with recipient
        (within 24 hours of threat)

Yes No—Student previously bullied the recipient

Victim or Recipient of Threat

Number of Victims:
☐ 1 ☐ 2 ☐ 3 ☐ 4 ☐ 5 or more

Primary Recipient:
☐ Student ☐ Teacher ☐ Parent
☐ Administrator ☐ Other: _____

Grade (if applicable): _____

Gender: ☐ M ☐ F

Race:
☐ Caucasian ☐ African Am. ☐ Hispanic
☐ Asian Am. ☐ Other: _____

Special Education (if applicable):
☐ LD ☐ OHI ☐ MR
☐ ED ☐ Other: _____

Yes No—Recipient witnessed the threat

Yes No—Recipient previously bullied the student

Evaluation of Threat (Use these questions as the interview foundation; modify them and use additional pages as needed.)

Student Interview

1. Do you know why I wanted to talk with you? Tell me.

   _____
   _____
   _____
   _____

2. What happened today when you were [place of incident]?

   _____
   _____
   _____
   _____

3. What exactly did you say? And what exactly did you do? (Write the student's exact words.)

   _____
   _____
   _____
   _____

4. What did you mean when you said or did that?

   _____
   _____
   _____
   _____

5. How do you think [person who was threatened] feels about what you said or did? (See if the student believes it frightened or intimidated the person who was threatened.)

   _____
   _____
   _____
   _____

6. What was the reason you said or did that? (Find out if there is a prior conflict or history to this threat.)

   _____
   _____
   _____
   _____

7. What are you going to do now that you have made this threat? (Ask if the student intends to carry out the threat.)

   _____
   _____
   _____
   _____

Witness Interview

☐ Recipient (target) of threat   or   ☐ Witness to threat, but not recipient

Witness name and grade or title: _____

1. What exactly happened today when you were [place of incident]?

    _____
    _____
    _____
    _____
    _____
    _____

2. What exactly did [student who made the threat] say or do? (Write the witness's exact words.)

    _____
    _____
    _____
    _____
    _____
    _____

3. What do you think he or she meant when saying or doing that?

    _____
    _____
    _____
    _____
    _____
    _____

4. How do you feel about what he or she said or did? (Gauge whether the person who observed or received the threat feels frightened or intimidated.) Are you concerned that he or she might actually do it?

    _____
    _____
    _____
    _____
    _____

5. Why did he or she say or do that? (Find out whether witness knows of any prior conflict or history behind this threat.)

    _____
    _____
    _____
    _____
    _____

Threat Responses

Disciplinary Action

Yes   No —Reprimanded student

Yes   No —Parent conference

Yes   No —In-school time-out

Yes   No —Detention (number of days): _____

Yes   No —Suspension (number of days): _____

Yes   No —Expulsion recommended

Yes   No —Other disciplinary action: _____

Interventions and Safety Precautions

Yes   No—Interviewed and advised student who made threat

Yes   No—Interviewed and advised student's parents

Yes   No—Consulted with one or more school staff members

Yes   No—Interviewed and advised other students

Yes   No—Law enforcement consulted

Yes   No—Law enforcement contact with the student who made the threat

        Consequence of legal action (probation, detention, release into parent's custody, etc.):

_____

_____

Yes   No—Student might be eligible for special education services; referred for evaluation

Yes   No—Student already receiving special education services; referred to the IEP team for review

Yes   No—Student referred for a 504 plan.

_____

_____

Yes   No—Mental health assessment conducted by school-based staff

Yes   No—Mental health assessment conducted by an outside agency (court, DSS, psychologist, etc.)

_____

Yes   No—Parents of the threat recipient notified of the threat

Yes   No—Conflict mediation

Yes   No—School-based counseling

Yes   No—Alter schedule of the student to increase supervision or minimize contact with the recipient

_____

_____

Yes   No—Alternative educational placement (alternative school, day treatment program, homebound, etc.)

Yes   No—Change in transportation (bus suspension, special transportation, etc.)

Yes   No—Inpatient mental health services

Yes   No—Outpatient mental health services (counseling or therapy with outside mental health provider)

Yes   No—Other safety precautions (please list):

_____

_____

BEHAVIOR SUPPORT PLAN

The Behavior Support Plan (BSP) form was developed by Diana Browning Wright for use anytime a student is in need of behavior support. The blank form is followed by three examples corresponding to the cases in Chapter 10. This form can be used with an Individualized Education Program (IEP), with a 504 plan, or in addressing a student's threat in the absence of an IEP or a 504 plan. Information on BSP training and the use of the BSP Quality Evaluation Guide is available at http://www.pent.ca.gov.

Behavior Support Plan

CONFIDENTIAL—FOR TEACHER OR STAFF USE ONLY

For behavior interfering with the student's learning or the learning of others

This BSP attaches to . . .

☐ IEP date: _____ ☐ 504 plan date: _____ ☐ Team meeting date: _____

Student name _____

Today's date _____ Next review date _____

1. The behavior impeding learning is . . . (Describe what it looks like.)
   _____
   _____

2. It impedes learning because . . .
   _____
   _____

3. The need for a BSP is ☐ early-stage intervention ☐ moderate ☐ serious ☐ extreme.

4. Frequency, intensity, or duration of behavior:
   _____

   ☐ reported by _____ ☐ observed by _____

PART I: PREVENTION—ENVIRONMENTAL FACTORS AND NEEDED CHANGES

5. What are the predictors for the behavior (situations in which the behavior is likely to occur—people, time, place, subject, etc.)?
   _____
   _____

6. What supports the student using the problem behavior? (What is missing or what needs changing in the environment or curriculum?)
   _____
   _____
   _____

Remove student's need to use the problem behavior.

7. What environmental changes, structure, and supports are recommended to remove the student's need to use this behavior?
   _____
   _____
   _____
   _____
   _____
   _____

   Who will establish the above? _____
   Who will monitor the above? _____

PART II: ALTERNATIVES—FUNCTIONAL FACTORS AND NEW BEHAVIORS TO SUPPORT

8. Team believes the behavior occurs because (function of behavior in terms of obtaining, protesting, or avoiding something):

   _____

   _____

Support an alternative behavior that meets same need.

9. What does the team believe the student should do instead of the problem behavior? (How should the student escape, protest, or avoid the behavior or get his or her need met in an acceptable way?)

   _____

   _____

   _____

10. What teaching strategies, curriculum, or materials are needed to teach the alternative behavior?

    _____

    _____

    _____

    _____

    By whom? _____

    How frequently? _____

    _____

11. What are reinforcers to use for establishing, maintaining, and generalizing the new behavior(s)?

    _____

    _____

    _____

    _____

    Selection of reinforcer based on . . .

    _____

    _____

    ☐ reinforcer for using replacement behavior ☐ reinforcer for general increase in positive behaviors

    By whom? _____

    How frequently? _____

    _____

PART III: REACTIONS—STRATEGIES FOR RESPONDING TO PROBLEM RECURRENCE

12. What strategies will be employed if the problem behavior occurs again (prompt student to switch to the replacement behavior, review negative consequences of undesirable behavior, etc.)?

    _____

    _____

    _____

    _____

    By whom? _____

PART IV: OUTCOME—BEHAVIORAL GOALS

13. Behavioral goal(s):

_____

_____

_____

_____

The above behavioral goal(s) is to . . .

☐ reduce frequency of problem behavior   ☐ increase use of replacement behavior

☐ develop new general skills that remove student's need to use the problem behavior

Conclusions

☐ Yes   ☐ No   Are curriculum accommodations or modifications also necessary?
If so, where are they described? _____

☐ Yes   ☐ No   Are environmental supports or changes necessary?

☐ Yes   ☐ No   Is reinforcement of alternative behavior alone enough? (No new teaching is necessary.)

☐ Yes   ☐ No   Are both teaching of new alternative behavior and reinforcement needed?

☐ Yes   ☐ No   Is this BSP to be coordinated with other agencies' service plans?

Person responsible for contact among agencies: _____

PART V: COMMUNICATION

Type and frequency of communication (all participants):

_____

_____

_____

_____

Among _____

How frequently? _____

_____

PART VI: PARTICIPANTS IN PLAN DEVELOPMENT

☐ Student _____

☐ Parent or guardian _____

☐ Educator and title _____

☐ Educator and title _____

☐ Educator and title _____

☐ Administrator _____

☐ Administrator _____

☐ Other _____

☐ Other _____

Behavior Support Plan—Case Example

For behavior interfering with the student's learning or the learning of others

This BSP attaches to . . .

☒ IEP date: __11-02__   ☐ 504 plan date: _____   ☐ Team meeting date: _____

Student name __Mitch Randolph__

Today's date __01-25__   Next review date __04-25__

1. The behavior impeding learning is . . . (Describe what it looks like.)
    a verbal threat made to three peers. "I might as well snuff myself and for that matter all of you with my dad's gun. I know where it is!"

2. It impedes learning because . . .
    Mitch is suicidal and unmotivated to learn. His threats distress and endanger other students and disrupt the learning environment.

3. The need for a BSP is ☐ early-stage intervention ☐ moderate ☒ serious ☐ extreme is.

4. Frequency, intensity, or duration of behavior
    One incident, ongoing depression

    ☒ reported by __peers__   ☐ observed by _____

PART I: PREVENTION—ENVIRONMENTAL FACTORS AND NEEDED CHANGES

5. What are the predictors for the behavior (situations in which the behavior is likely to occur—people, time, place, subject, etc.)?
    Alone with peers and no adult supervision. Recent loss of parent.

6. What supports the student using the problem behavior? (What is missing or what needs changing in the environment or curriculum?)
    Mitch has not participated in counseling to deal with grief and anger following the loss of his father.
    Mitch does not have a strong supportive relationship with a member of the school staff whom he can contact when feeling distressed.

Remove student's need to use the problem behavior.

7. What environmental changes, structure, and supports are recommended to remove the student's need to use this behavior?
    To help Mitch become more successful in his classes, teachers agree that academic tasks should be broken into smaller segments with frequent reinforcement and encouragement. To improve adult monitoring and support, Mitch will maintain regular contact with the counselor. Teachers will refer Mitch to the counselor, Mrs. Jay, anytime he appears unusually withdrawn or makes a statement indicating hopelessness or distress. If Mitch's counselor is absent, Mitch agrees to check in with Mr. Josephson, his homeroom teacher. Mr. James (math teacher) stated that Mitch is interested in chess, and he will invite Mitch to join the chess club, which he sponsors.

    Who will establish the above? __Counselors or teachers__

    Who will monitor the above? __Teachers will report on his academic status weekly to the__ principal. The counselor will report on Mitch's depression weekly to the principal and will call his mother whenever there is any significant change.

PART II: ALTERNATIVES—FUNCTIONAL FACTORS AND NEW BEHAVIORS TO SUPPORT

8. Team believes the behavior occurs because (function of behavior in terms of obtaining, protesting, or avoiding something):

   Mitch expressed his distress and feelings of alienation over his recent loss by threatening to hurt himself or others. In this state, he is oversensitive to frustration and rejection by his peers.

Support an alternative behavior that meets same need.

9. What does the team believe the student should do instead of the problem behavior? (How should the student escape, protest, or avoid the behavior or get his or her need met in an acceptable way?)

   Encourage Mitch to express his feelings in counseling sessions and with his mother. Teach Mitch how to respond to frustration with his peers without making a threat.

10. What teaching strategies, curriculum, or materials are needed to teach the alternative behavior?

    Mitch has the verbal skills to learn alternative ways to express himself, if encouraged by staff. His mother has requested that he discuss his concerns about his father with the minister of their church. The school counselor will maintain close communication with Mitch and his mother to monitor his progress and safety.

    By whom?   Church minister, Rev. Jameson

    How frequently?   The counselor will check with Mitch daily for the next two weeks and then twice per week and will call his mother as needed.

11. What are reinforcers to use for establishing, maintaining, and generalizing the new behavior(s)?

    Teachers will praise and encourage evidence of positive engagement in school and report his progress to the counselor, who will report to his mother and outside therapist. During daily check-in procedures, the counselor will demonstrate empathy and support, providing oral praise for increased engagement and resolving hopelessness feelings.

    Selection of reinforcer based on . . .

    Mitch has a history of responding to encouragement and praise from adults.

    ☐ reinforcer for using replacement behavior   ☒ reinforcer for general increase in positive behaviors

    By whom?   Counselor and teachers

    How frequently?   Daily

PART III: REACTIONS—STRATEGIES FOR RESPONDING TO PROBLEM RECURRENCE

12. What strategies will be employed if the problem behavior occurs again (prompt student to switch to the replacement behavior, review negative consequences of undesirable behavior, etc.)?

    Encourage peers to seek help for Mitch by reporting any expressions of hopelessness or thoughts of dying or of hurting others. Mitch agrees to contact his outside therapist, school counselor, or both if hopelessness reoccurs. Standard school policy will be followed if another threat to harm himself or others is expressed. (The range of responses likely to be considered in the assessment process: disciplinary removal, expulsion, referral to police, intensified therapeutic interventions [e.g., hospitalization].)

    By whom?   Counselor and teacher

PART IV: OUTCOME—BEHAVIORAL GOALS

13. Behavioral goal(s):

By 04/25, Mitch will have participated in all required check-ins with the counselor. He will demonstrate increased involvement in school through involvement in the chess club or another group on a weekly basis. He will be able to express more positive feelings about himself and be able to describe positive and worthwhile aspects of his life. He will not make any statements of intent to harm himself or others.

The above behavioral goal(s) is to . . .

☒ reduce frequency of problem behavior　　☒ increase use of replacement behavior

☐ develop new general skills that remove student's need to use the problem behavior

Conclusions

☒ Yes　☐ No　Are curriculum accommodations or modifications also necessary?

If so, where are they described? _____

☒ Yes　☐ No　Are environmental supports or changes necessary?

☐ Yes　☒ No　Is reinforcement of alternative behavior alone enough? (No new teaching is necessary.)

☒ Yes　☐ No　Are both teaching of new alternative behavior and reinforcement needed?

☒ Yes　☐ No　Is this BSP to be coordinated with other agencies' service plans?

Person responsible for contact among agencies: The counselor is to contact Mitch's outside therapist twice per month until it is agreed that the problem is resolved.

PART V: COMMUNICATION

Type and frequency of communication (all participants):

Mitch's mother, his outside therapist, and the principal are to receive weekly verbal progress reports from the counselor for one month, and then the frequency will be reduced if appropriate. His teachers are to contact the counselor or principal if any behaviors suggesting despair or alienation are observed. CONTACT MUST BE ON THE SAME DAY. The counselor is to coordinate follow-up and to communicate back to staff.

Among Mother, counselor, principal, and therapist

How frequently? Weekly for one month and then reevaluate frequently

PART VI: PARTICIPANTS IN PLAN DEVELOPMENT

☒ Student　Mitch

☒ Parent or guardian　Mrs. Randolph

☒ Educator and title　Mrs. Marbury, school psychologist

☒ Educator and title　Ms. Evans, lead teacher

☒ Educator and title　Mrs. Jay, counselor

☒ Administrator　Ms. Adams, assistant principal

☒ Administrator　Ms. Holt, principal

☒ Other　Rev. Jameson, minister

☒ Other　Officer Monroe, school resource officer

For behavior interfering with the student's learning or the learning of others

This BSP attaches to . . .

☒ IEP date: _03-04_   ☐ 504 plan date: _____   ☐ Team meeting date: _____

Student name _Ramon Santiago_

Today's date _03-04_ _____   Next review date _06-04_ _____

1. The behavior impeding learning is . . . (Describe what it looks like.)
    Ramon allegedly told a peer, "I'll have my homeboys kill you" during PE.

2. It impedes learning because . . .
    threats create fear and impede safe, orderly learning environments.

3. The need for a BSP is ☐ early-stage intervention   ☐ moderate   ☒ serious   ☐ extreme is.

4. Frequency, intensity, or duration of behavior
    Ramon has made one very serious threat. (Note: He has had 12 disciplinary referrals this year, including
    wearing at teachers, physical fighting, and refusing to cooperate with teachers—see disciplinary file.)

    ☒ reported by _classmate who was threatened_   ☒ observed by _other students interviewed by Officer Ramirez_

PART I: PREVENTION—ENVIRONMENTAL FACTORS AND NEEDED CHANGES

5. What are the predictors for the behavior (situations in which the behavior is likely to occur—
    people, time, place, subject, etc.)?
    Ramon's aggressive behavior usually occurs when there are peers watching and encouraging aggression. Peers
    were present when he made the threat.

6. What supports the student using the problem behavior? (What is missing or what needs changing in
    the environment or curriculum?)
    In Ramon's neighborhood and school, there are negative peer models who support "acting tough" and defying
    authority. These peers are reported to be gang members. Ramon has not yet formed relationships with peers who
    value achievement and appropriate nonviolent interactions.

Remove student's need to use the problem behavior.

7. What environmental changes, structure, and supports are recommended to remove the student's
    need to use this behavior?
    Ramon will attend a school in which he is separated from his current peer group and can attend counseling
    groups led by former gang members for the purpose of discouraging gang involvement. Teachers and counselors
    will use shaping of positive behaviors to promote better classroom behavior.

    Who will establish the above? _Counselor and teacher_

    Who will monitor the above? _Principal and counselor_

PART II: ALTERNATIVES—FUNCTIONAL FACTORS AND NEW BEHAVIORS TO SUPPORT

8. Team believes the behavior occurs because (function of behavior in terms of obtaining, protesting, or avoiding something):

   Ramon desires gang affiliation in order to achieve status and recognition.

Support an alternative behavior that meets same need.

9. What does the team believe the student should do instead of the problem behavior? (How should the student escape, protest, or avoid the behavior or get his or her need met in an acceptable way?)

   Ramon needs to learn how to achieve recognition using positive behavior. He also needs instruction on resisting peer pressure and resolving peer conflicts. He could benefit from a positive relationship with a mentor who gives him an alternative source of acceptance and recognition.

10. What teaching strategies, curriculum, or materials are needed to teach the alternative behavior?

    Ramon will participate in small group sessions to learn appropriate conflict resolution strategies and how to resist peer pressure. The group will use the GREAT gang resistance materials, the New Horizons School handbook, and the Boys Town Model program materials for dangerous students. He will also have one-on-one mentoring designed to discourage and replace gang involvement.

    By whom? Site teacher, group leader, and mentor

    How frequently? Daily group meetings, with mentor meetings at least twice weekly

11. What are reinforcers to use for establishing, maintaining, and generalizing the new behavior(s)?

    If Ramon demonstrates evidence of positive interactions with peers, mentors, and staff, he will receive points toward privileges in the school and a note to take home describing his successes to his parents. He will receive daily encouragement and recognition through participation in group sessions.

    Selection of reinforcer based on . . .

    Ramon participating in the development of this plan and agreeing that he is willing to try it. He would like to earn the approval of his parents and earn the privileges associated with the new school.

    ☒ reinforcer for using replacement behavior   ☒ reinforcer for general increase in positive behaviors

    By whom? Site teacher, group leader, and mentor

    How frequently? Daily

PART III: REACTIONS—STRATEGIES FOR RESPONDING TO PROBLEM RECURRENCE

12. What strategies will be employed if the problem behavior occurs again (prompt student to switch to the replacement behavior, review negative consequences of undesirable behavior, etc.)?

    1. Remind Ramon of appropriate conflict resolution steps if he is beginning to escalate his behavior.

    2. If Ramon uses inappropriate language and engages in verbal aggression, but not a threat, the counselors will engage him in the "inappropriate behavior" debriefing steps as outlined in the New Horizons guidebook.

    3. If Ramon threatens a peer, the adult should use standard crisis-intervention procedures and call for assistance from the administration. The threat assessment team and probation officer should be notified. If Ramon poses a threat, these steps will likely include the police, the probation officer, and district disciplinary actions, including removal to a more restrictive setting.

    By whom? Site counselor, teacher, and probation officer

PART IV: OUTCOME—BEHAVIORAL GOALS

13. Behavioral goal(s):

By 06/04, Ramon will exhibit three positive statements to his peers during counseling sessions and in classroom activities as observed, rated, and charted by teachers and counselors using the New Horizons positive behaviors checklist, on 90% of daily observations. By 06/04, Ramon will demonstrate the steps in nonviolent conflict resolution taught to him by his mentor with 90% accuracy in at least three out of four role-play situations as observed and rated by the mentor.

The above behavioral goal(s) is to . . .

☐ reduce frequency of problem behavior   ☒ increase use of replacement behavior

☒ develop new general skills that remove student's need to use the problem behavior

Conclusions

☒ Yes   ☐ No   Are curriculum accommodations or modifications also necessary?
If so, where are they described? _____

☒ Yes   ☐ No   Are environmental supports or changes necessary?

☐ Yes   ☒ No   Is reinforcement of alternative behavior alone enough? (No new teaching is necessary.)

☒ Yes   ☐ No   Are both teaching of new alternative behavior and reinforcement needed?

☒ Yes   ☐ No   Is this BSP to be coordinated with other agencies' service plans?

Person responsible for contact among agencies: Principal and counselor report to the probation officer.

PART V: COMMUNICATION

Type and frequency of communication (all participants):

Teachers or the counselor and the mentor will collaborate on a weekly progress report for the principal, parents, and probation officer. Any "inappropriate behavior" work sheets will be shared with parents. All recipients will communicate recommendations back to the counselor.

Among   Teachers, counselor, parents, and probation officer

How frequently?   Weekly; immediately if a threat or violence is involved

PART VI: PARTICIPANTS IN PLAN DEVELOPMENT

☒ Student   Ramon Santiago

☒ Parent or guardian   Mr. and Mrs. Santiago

☒ Educator and title   Mr. Sanchez, mentor and counselor

☒ Educator and title   Mrs. Robinson, school psychologist

☒ Educator and title   Mr. Johnson, teacher

☒ Administrator   Mr. Jackson, assistant principal

☒ Administrator   Mrs. Wright, principal of interim alternative setting

☒ Other   Mr. Alison, probation officer

☒ Other   Officer Ramirez

Behavior Support Plan—Case Example CONFIDENTIAL—FOR TEACHER OR STAFF USE ONLY

For behavior interfering with the student's learning or the learning of others

This BSP attaches to . . .

☐ IEP date: _____ ☐ 504 plan date: _____ ☒ Team meeting date: 02/20

Student name Carlie Kim

Today's date 02/20 Next review date 05/20

1. The behavior impeding learning is . . . (Describe what it looks like.)

    in response to a peer's criticism of her shoes, "Those shoes look really dead," Carlie replied, "Maybe you
    should be dead!" and pointed a pair of scissors at the peer. The peer and others interpreted Carlie's behavior
    as a threat.

2. It impedes learning because . . .

    Teasing and threatening behavior interfere with normal classroom functioning and are not conducive to learning.

3. The need for a BSP is ☐ early stage intervention ☐ moderate ☒ serious ☐ extreme is.

4. Frequency, intensity, or duration of behavior

    Only one threat

    ☒ reported by teachers   ☒ observed by peers

PART I: PREVENTION—ENVIRONMENTAL FACTORS AND NEEDED CHANGES

5. What are the predictors for the behavior (situations in which the behavior is likely to occur—
    people, time, place, subject, etc.)?

    Carlie felt teased and criticized by her peers.

6. What supports the student using the problem behavior? (What is missing or what needs changing in
    the environment or curriculum?)

    Carlie needs help learning how to deal with teasing and social bullying. Her peers need instruction that
    teasing and social bullying are not acceptable.

Remove student's need to use the problem behavior.

7. What environmental changes, structure, and supports are recommended to remove the student's
    need to use this behavior?

    Carlie and her peers need help in interacting without teasing and bullying. This problem will be addressed
    by counseling Carlie and her peers and through the school's bully prevention curriculum that is taught in
    ninth grade health class. Carlie's teachers will monitor her peer interactions and respond to any social
    bullying or teasing.

    Who will establish the above? Ninth grade teacher and social worker

    Who will monitor the above? Teacher and social worker

PART II: ALTERNATIVES—FUNCTIONAL FACTORS AND NEW BEHAVIORS TO SUPPORT

8. Team believes the behavior occurs because (function of behavior in terms of obtaining, protesting, or avoiding something):

    Carlie protested being teased by making a threat.

Support an alternative behavior that meets same need.

9. What does the team believe the student should do instead of the problem behavior? (How should the student escape, protest, or avoid the behavior or get his or her need met in an acceptable way?)

    Carlie should learn how to tell someone to stop teasing her without making a threat.

10. What teaching strategies, curriculum, or materials are needed to teach the alternative behavior?

    Carlie will learn responses to bullying and teasing with the counselor in individual and small group sessions.
    The curriculum will be taken from Don't Laugh at Me and Bully-Proofing Your School. Carlie's peers require
    antibullying instruction, which will occur in ninth grade health class. The ninth grade health teacher will
    inservice other teachers on how to teach peers to stop being passive bystanders and take a more active role in
    reinforcing "no put-downs!"

    By whom?   Teachers and social worker

    How frequently?   Carlie's sessions will be twice per week for 20 minutes until the next team meeting.
    Ninth grade health class instruction will be three times per week for two weeks of antibullying instruction.

11. What are reinforcers to use for establishing, maintaining, and generalizing the new behavior(s)?

    Carlie will receive praise from staff for using appropriate protests if she is teased again.

    Selection of reinforcer based on . . .

    Carlie's motivation by teacher praise and desire to learn how to cope with teasing.

    ☒ reinforcer for using replacement behavior   ☐ reinforcer for general increase in positive behaviors

    By whom?   Teachers and social worker

    How frequently?   When observed by staff or reported by Charlie.

PART III: REACTIONS—STRATEGIES FOR RESPONDING TO PROBLEM RECURRENCE

12. What strategies will be employed if the problem behavior occurs again (prompt student to switch to the replacement behavior, review negative consequences of undesirable behavior, etc.)?

    If Carlie does not show appropriate responses to teasing, interrupt the interaction and remind everyone of
    their expected behavior. Follow up with Carlie in private to remind her of her agreement to use appropriate
    statements in responding to teasing. If Carlie makes another threat, immediately separate her from other
    students and notify the threat assessment team. If Carlie engages in physically aggressive behavior, follow
    district procedures for nonviolent crisis intervention and obtain immediate staff support from principal's
    office or school resource officer.

    By whom?   Teacher, social worker, threat assessment team, and school resource officer

PART IV: OUTCOME—BEHAVIORAL GOALS

13. Behavioral goal(s):

By 05/20, Carlie will (1) have made no threats to anyone and (2) have written in her counseling journal each week about any situation where she was teased, or worried she might be teased, so that she can review it with her counselor.

The above behavioral goal(s) is to . . .

☒ reduce frequency of problem behavior   ☒ increase use of replacement behavior

☒ develop new general skills that remove student's need to use the problem behavior

Conclusions

☐ Yes   ☒ No   Are curriculum accommodations or modifications also necessary?
If so, where are they described? _____

☒ Yes   ☐ No   Are environmental supports or changes necessary?

☐ Yes   ☒ No   Is reinforcement of alternative behavior alone enough? (No new teaching is necessary.)

☒ Yes   ☐ No   Are both teaching of new alternative behavior and reinforcement needed?

☐ Yes   ☒ No   Is this BSP to be coordinated with other agencies' service plans?

Person responsible for contact among agencies: not applicable

PART V: COMMUNICATION

Type and frequency of communication (all participants):

(1) Carlie will meet with her counselor weekly or after another teasing incident. (2) Any school staff observing teasing will report it to her teacher or counselor. (3) Any threatening behavior will be reported to the threat assessment team immediately. (4) The counselor will speak with parents weekly to update them on her progress. (5) Teachers will report any major change in Carlie's behavior or demeanor to her social worker.

Among? Counselor and the student, her parents, and her teacher

How frequently? At least weekly

PART VI: PARTICIPANTS IN PLAN DEVELOPMENT

☒ Student Carlie Kim

☒ Parent or guardian Mr. and Mrs. Kim

☒ Educator and title Ms. Evans, teacher

☒ Educator and title Mr. Burwald, teacher

☒ Educator and title Mr. Cornwall, school psychologist

☒ Administrator Mrs. Behrens, principal

☒ Administrator Mr. Brown, social worker

☒ Other Officer Martin

☐ Other _____

Test Your Knowledge of These Guidelines

What Is the Most Likely Threat Classification?

Choose one of four options:

1	An angry student says, "I'm gonna kill you." On interview, the student says he has no plans to harm the classmate and that he just lost his temper. He agrees to apologize. a. No threat b. Transient threat c. Serious substantive threat d. Very serious substantive threat
2	Two students argue, and one punches the other. On interview, the student says he should not have lost his temper but that he acted in self-defense. a. No threat b. Transient threat c. Serious substantive threat d. Very serious substantive threat
3	A student tells a friend that he will beat up someone in the parking lot after school. On interview, the student is uncooperative and says that what he does after school is his own business. a. No threat b. Transient threat c. Serious substantive threat d. Very serious substantive threat
4	A student is found with a list of student names under the heading "Scheduled to Die." On interview, the student is sullen and quiet. You do not believe he was simply trying to get attention. a. No threat b. Transient threat c. Serious substantive threat d. Very serious substantive threat
5	A student has a list of student names under the heading "Punks to Beat Up." On interview, the student describes feeling angry at his peers and perceives them as laughing at him all the time. He says that he wasn't going to really hurt anyone, but he has a history of fighting. a. No threat b. Transient threat c. Serious substantive threat d. Very serious substantive threat

6	A student tells two friends that she is going to stab another student. On interview, the student says, "Well, she deserves it!" a. No threat b. Transient threat c. Serious substantive threat d. Very serious substantive threat
7	A student says he is going to sodomize another student in the bathroom. On interview, the student is defiant, saying that it is none of your business. a. No threat b. Transient threat c. Serious substantive threat d. Very serious substantive threat
8	A student says she's going to break both legs of a student for beating her in a race. On interview, the student contends that she was joking. "This is just how we talk. We were all laughing." a. No threat b. Transient threat c. Serious substantive threat d. Very serious substantive threat
9	A student calls in a bomb threat. No bomb is found, and he knows nothing about bombs. On interview, the student explains that he just wanted to see what would happen. "I was joking." a. No threat b. Transient threat c. Serious substantive threat d. Very serious substantive threat
10	A student screams obscene insults at a teacher and then storms out of the classroom. On interview, the student says that the teacher isn't fair. a. No threat b. Transient threat c. Serious substantive threat d. Very serious substantive threat
11	A student turns in an English essay that describes a violent scene from a war. On interview, the student says that his uncle is fighting in the Middle East. a. No threat b. Transient threat c. Serious substantive threat d. Very serious substantive threat

12	A student says a bully is threatening to beat him up at the bus stop after school. On interview, the accused student denies making a threat. You aren't sure who is telling the truth. a. No threat b. Transient threat c. Serious substantive threat d. Very serious substantive threat
13	A fourth grade student tells a classmate that he is going to burn down the school. On interview, the student denies making the statement. His teacher has seen him drawing a map of the school and knows he is upset over being disciplined in the classroom. a. No threat b. Transient threat c. Serious substantive threat d. Very serious substantive threat
14	A second grade student threatens to stab a classmate with a pair of scissors. On interview, the student says she was just joking and wouldn't hurt anyone. a. No threat b. Transient threat c. Serious substantive threat d. Very serious substantive threat
15	A parent says that three students who are part of a gang threatened to beat up her son for walking down their street on the way to school. On interview, the boy denies being threatened. The three students deny making a threat. You know they belong to a ganglike group and doubt they are telling the truth. a. No threat b. Transient threat c. Serious substantive threat d. Very serious substantive threat
16	A student is reported to have a Web site containing threats to "blow away" several classmates. On interview, the student says the Web site is just a joke. He says he has the right to free speech on the Internet. His classmates say they are worried he will do something to hurt them. a. No threat b. Transient threat c. Serious substantive threat d. Very serious substantive threat

What Is the Most Likely Threat Classification?

ANSWERS

1	An angry student says, "I'm gonna kill you." The threat has been resolved with the student's explanation and apology. b. Transient threat
2	Two students argue, and one punches the other. The student has assaulted his classmate, but he has not expressed an intent to harm him in the future, so no threat has been made. a. No threat
3	A student tells a friend that he will beat up someone in the parking lot after school. The threat is not resolved and has a designated time and place, so it is substantive. It involves beating up someone, so it is serious. c. Serious substantive threat
4	A student is found with a list of student names under the heading "Scheduled to Die." The threat is not resolved. Because you are uncertain, treat the threat as substantive. A homicidal threat is very serious. d. Very serious substantive threat
5	A student has a list of student names under the heading "Punks to Beat Up." The threat is not resolved, so it is substantive. The threat involves an assault, so it is serious. c. Serious substantive threat
6	A student tells two friends that she is going to stab another student. The threat is not resolved, so it must be considered substantive. It may involve injury with a weapon, so it is very serious. d. Very serious substantive threat
7	A student says he is going to sodomize another student in the bathroom. The threat is not resolved, so it must be considered substantive. It involves a sexual assault, so it is very serious. d. Very serious substantive threat
8	A student says she's going to break both legs of a student for beating her in a race. This threat is likely to be transient, if the student's account is confirmed by others. b. Transient threat
9	A student calls in a bomb threat. No bomb is found, and he knows nothing about bombs. The threat involves a serious crime, but it is a transient threat because there is no intention to set off a bomb. b. Transient threat
10	A student screams obscene insults at a teacher and then storms out of the classroom. Although his behavior is a serious disciplinary violation, the student has not expressed a threat. a. No threat
11	A student turns in an English essay that describes a violent scene from a war. The student has not expressed a threat. a. No threat

12	A student says a bully is threatening to beat him up at the bus stop after school. If in doubt, treat the threat as substantive. The threat involves an assault, so it is serious. c. Serious substantive threat
13	A fourth grade student tells a classmate that he is going to burn down the school. A fourth grade student is capable of setting a fire, and there is evidence of planning. A threat to burn down a building is very serious because of the potential for severe injury or death. d. Very serious substantive threat
14	A second grade student threatens to stab a classmate with a pair of scissors. Although the threat involves a weapon, if others confirm that the threat was made in a joking manner, the threat is most likely to be transient. b. Transient threat
15	A parent says that three students who are part of a gang threatened to beat up her son for walking down their street on the way to school. The student is probably afraid to admit being threatened. Whenever in doubt, treat a threat as substantive. The involvement of a gang raises concern. A threat to assault someone is serious, unless you had reason to suspect the beating would cause severe injury, in which case a classification of "very serious" would be justified. c. Serious substantive threat
16	A student is reported to have a Web site containing threats to "blow away" several classmates. The threat has not been resolved so it should be considered substantive and, because it involves a threat to kill, it is very serious. d. Very serious substantive threat

What Is the Next Step?

Choose the appropriate option or options:

1	An angry student says, "I'm gonna kill you." Now that the threat has been resolved as transient, what is the next thing to do? a. Take no further action. b. Suspend the student for 5 days. c. Refer the student for a mental health assessment. d. Refer the two students for conflict mediation
2	Two students argue, and one punches the other. The student has assaulted his classmate, but he has not expressed an intent to harm him in the future, so no threat has been made. The student admitted that he should not have lost his temper but acted in self-defense. Is there anything else to do? a. Take no further action. b. Discipline the student for punching a peer. c. Interview the students to determine if they still want to fight. d. Refer the two students for conflict mediation.
3	A student tells a friend that he will beat up someone in the parking lot after school. The student was uncooperative, and you classified the case as a serious substantive threat. What else do you do? a. Notify the intended victim and the victim's parents. b. Ask the school police officer to arrest the student. c. Refer the student for a mental health assessment. d. Take protective action by notifying the student's parents and having them take their son home after school.
4	A student is found with a list of student names under the heading "Scheduled to Die." The student was sullen and uncooperative, and you did not believe the student was joking or simply trying to get attention. The threat also involved a felonious assault, so you classified the threat as a very serious substantive threat. What should you do? a. Refer the student for a mental health assessment. b. Notify the intended victims and the victims' parents. c. Consult with law enforcement. d. Expel the student for his plans to carry out a very serious substantive threat.
5	A student has a list of student names under the heading "Punks to Beat Up." Because the problem did not seem to be resolved and it involved a plan to assault someone, the threat was classified as a serious substantive threat. What can you do? a. Refer the student for a mental health assessment. b. Notify the intended victims and the victims' parents. c. Refer the student for counseling. d. Take protective action by keeping the student in the principal's office until his parents pick him up.

6	A student tells two friends that she is going to stab another student. Considering this threat was not resolved and involved potential injury with a weapon, you classified it as a very serious substantive threat. Now what are some steps you should take? a. Search the student's locker to see if she has a weapon. b. Refer the students for peer mediation. c. Notify the intended victim and the victim's parents. d. Take protective action by having the police arrest the student.
7	A student says he is going to sodomize another student in the bathroom. Because the threat was not resolved and involved a potential sexual assault, it was classified as a very serious substantive threat. What are your options? a. Refer the student for a mental health assessment. b. Refer the students for peer mediation. c. Notify the intended victim and the victim's parents. d. Suspend the student until he is willing to explain himself.
8	A student says she's going to break both legs of a student for beating her in a race. The student's claim that she was joking was confirmed by other witnesses, and the threat was classified as transient. What do you do next? a. Refer the student for counseling. b. Refer the students for peer mediation. c. Take no further action. d. Interview the other student to gain her perspective.
9	A student calls in a bomb threat. No bomb is found, and he knows nothing about bombs. When questioned, the student claimed that he had no intention of actually setting off bombs in the school. With this information, you classified the threat as transient. What else must be done? a. Report the incident to the police to search the student's home. b. Refer the student for immediate counseling. c. Take legal and disciplinary action. d. In a brief letter, inform parents of the situation and the security measures taken.
10	A student screams obscene insults at a teacher and then storms out of the classroom. The student has a history of angry outbursts and conflict with this teacher, and he has claimed that the teacher does not treat him fairly. However, no threat has been made. What actions should be taken? a. Take no further action. b. Refer the student for counseling. c. Refer the student for special education evaluation. d. Interview the student.

11	A student turns in an English essay that describes a violent scene from a war. He is a good student who writes descriptive essays. He admires his uncle who is fighting in the Middle East. No threat has been made, so what do you do? a. Take no further action. b. Refer him to counseling to help him realize that fighting is not something to be respected. c. Notify his parents of the content of his essay. d. Discipline the student for expressing violent content in a school assignment.
12	A student says a bully is threatening to beat him up at the bus stop after school. He said the bully has threatened him several other times this year, but he was too afraid to say anything. The other student claimed that he has never threatened him. You were unsure about who to believe, but you classified the threat as a serious substantive one because it involves an assault. What should you do next? a. Notify both of the students' parents. b. Take protective action by keeping both boys in the principal's office until their parents come to get them. c. Refer both boys for mental health assessments to determine who is lying. d. Refer the boys for peer mediation.
13	A fourth grade student tells a classmate that he is going to burn down the school. Considering the student's refusal to admit he made the threat despite the evidence of planning, you classified the threat as a very serious substantive threat. Where do you go from here? a. Refer the student for a mental health assessment. b. Suspend the student until he is deemed safe for school. c. Take protective action by notifying the student's parents and having them pick him up. d. Ask the police to arrest the student.
14	A second grade student threatens to stab a classmate with a pair of scissors. The student's friends confirmed that her statement was a joke, and the classmate who was threatened did not feel the student would actually carry out the threat. The threat was classified as transient. Should you do anything else? a. Refer the two students for peer mediation. b. Notify the intended victim's parents. c. Take no protective action. d. Refer the student for character education training.
15	A parent says that three students who are part of a gang threatened to beat up her son for walking down their street on the way to school. When interviewed, the student denied that any threat was made and requested that the three students not be disciplined. Not knowing what to believe, but realizing the threat involved an assault, you classified it as a serious substantive threat. Now what should you do? a. Involve law enforcement to investigate the matter. b. Refer all students involved for peer mediation. c. Take no further action. d. Take protective action by keeping all students in school until their parents pick them up.

16	A student is reported to have a Web site containing threats to "blow away" several classmates. After being caught, the student continued to claim that he has the freedom to say whatever he wants on the Web site and that it is none of the school's business. Considering the threat was not resolved and it involved a threat to kill, you classified it as a very serious substantive threat. What course of action should you take? a. Notify the intended victims and their parents. b. Refer the student for a mental health assessment. c. Have the police search the student to determine whether he has a weapon. d. Expel the student for his plans to harm his classmates and his refusal to discuss the issue.

What Is the Next Step?

ANSWERS

1	An angry student says, "I'm gonna kill you." Because the student explained that he had no intention of harming his classmate and agreed to apologize, no protective action needs to be taken. However, it may be appropriate to refer the students to a counselor for conflict mediation. Depending on your school's disciplinary code, some disciplinary consequences may be appropriate as well. d. Refer the two students for conflict mediation.
2	Two students argue, and one punches the other. Although the student acted in self-defense, he should be disciplined for punching the other student. It is also important to determine if there is remaining tension or hostility between the two students and refer them for mediation to work out their problems. b. Discipline the student for punching a peer. c. Interview the students to determine if they still want to fight. d. Refer the two students for conflict mediation.
3	A student tells a friend that he will beat up someone in the parking lot after school. The threat is not serious enough to require a mental health assessment, and the student cannot be arrested because no crime has been committed. However, the intended victim and his parents should be notified, and safety measures should be taken to prevent the threat from being carried out. a. Notify the intended victim and the victim's parents. d. Take protective action by notifying the student's parents and having them take their son home after school.
4	A student is found with a list of student names under the heading "Scheduled to Die." All students who make very serious substantive threats should be referred for a mental health assessment. Law enforcement should be notified of any very serious substantive threat. The intended victims and their parents should also be notified so that they are aware of what is going on and know that the school is handling the situation in an appropriate manner. Without further investigation, the student should not be expelled. a. Refer the student for a mental health assessment. b. Notify the intended victims and the victims' parents. c. Consult with law enforcement.
5	A student has a list of student names under the heading "Punks to Beat Up." Considering this student's history of fighting, he should be referred for counseling. Because he could carry out this threat, you should take protective action and notify the parents of intended victims. b. Notify the intended victims and the victims' parents. c. Refer the student for counseling. d. Take protective action by keeping the student in the principal's office until his parents pick him up.

6	A student tells two friends that she is going to stab another student. Because this is a very serious substantive threat, peer mediation will not be adequate. A mental health assessment should be conducted. The school has the authority to search the student's locker to determine whether this threat is likely to be carried out. Although protective action should be taken, the police are unlikely to arrest the student if no crime has been committed. Instead, the school should supervise the student until her parents come to pick her up. a. Search the student's locker to see if she has a weapon. c. Notify the intended victim and the victim's parents.
7	A student says he is going to sodomize another student in the bathroom. This very serious substantive threat requires a mental health assessment and notification of the victim and his parents. The student might be suspended for disciplinary reasons or for safety reasons but probably not as a means of forcing him to give an explanation of his behavior. a. Refer the student for a mental health assessment. c. Notify the intended victim and the victim's parents.
8	A student says she's going to break both legs of a student for beating her in a race. It is important to learn of the intended victim's perspective. If she confirms that it was a joke and the threat was not taken seriously, no further action needs to be taken. d. Interview the other student to gain her perspective.
9	A student calls in a bomb threat. No bomb is found, and he knows nothing about bombs. Although it is only a transient threat, the incident was a serious violation of school code and a criminal act. Therefore, report the student to the police. The police will investigate further by searching the student's home to determine if there is any evidence of a bomb. All parents of students should be informed to quell unnecessary alarm and distress over the situation. c. Take legal and disciplinary action. d. In a brief letter, inform parents of the situation and the security measures taken.
10	A student screams obscene insults at a teacher and then storms out of the classroom. Considering the history of outbursts, it may be appropriate to refer the student for counseling. Prior to that, it is important to interview the student to discover what is going on with him. (Of course, discipline is an appropriate response, but that was not a listed option because it would make the question too easy!) b. Refer the student for counseling. d. Interview the student.
11	A student turns in an English essay that describes a violent scene from a war. Considering he has never been a problem student and the context in which he wrote the essay, there is no reason to take further action. a. Take no further action.

12	A student says a bully is threatening to beat him up at the bus stop after school. Although it is difficult to determine who is telling the truth, there is likely underlying hostility between the boys and a probability that the threat may be carried out. Peer mediation would not be appropriate in this case (see the bullying FAQ in Chapter 7). A mental health assessment would also not be appropriate because it is not a very serious substantive threat, but it is necessary to take protective action and notify both of the students' parents and have them pick the students up. a. Notify both of the students' parents. b. Take protective action by keeping both boys in the principal's office until their parents come to get them.
13	A fourth grade student tells a classmate that he is going to burn down the school. A mental health assessment is required because a very serious substantive threat has been made. He may be suspended pending a safety evaluation that includes a mental health assessment. Although he would not be arrested by the police, protective action can be taken by having his parents pick him up. a. Refer the student for a mental health assessment. b. Suspend the student until he is deemed safe for school. c. Take protective action by notifying the student's parents and having them pick him up.
14	A second grade student threatens to stab a classmate with a pair of scissors. Because the intended victim did not feel threatened and other classmates confirmed that it was a joke, there is no need for protective action or conflict mediation. The student should be admonished and instructed not to make jokes in this way. c. Take no protective action.
15	A parent says that three students who are part of a gang threatened to beat up her son for walking down their street on the way to school. Although the student claims that he has not been threatened, it is important to involve law enforcement to investigate the matter. Considering the possibility of gang involvement, peer mediation would not be appropriate, but some other form of mediation might be considered. It would be sensible to keep the students in school until their parents pick them up. a. Involve law enforcement to investigate the matter. d. Take protective action by keeping all students in school until their parents pick them up.
16	A student is reported to have a Web site containing threats to "blow away" several classmates. Because a very serious substantive threat has been made, the student should be given a mental health assessment, and the victims and their parents should be notified. The police should be involved, but they would not be able to search the student without probable cause. See the FAQ on student searches in Chapter 7. a. Notify the intended victims and their parents. b. Refer the student for a mental health assessment.

Advancement Project, and The Civil Rights Project (2000). *Opportunities suspended: The devastating consequences of zero tolerance and school discipline policies.* Boston: The Harvard Civil Rights Project. Available: http://www. civilrightsproject.harvard.edu/ research/discipline/opport_suspended.php.

Amato, J. M., & Cornell, D. (2003). How do youth claiming gang membership differ from youth who claim membership in another group, such as a crew, clique, posse, or mob? *Journal of Gang Research, 10,* 13–23.

American Psychological Association (1999). *Warning signs.* Washington, DC: Author.

Atkinson, A. (1997). *Virginia school resource officer handbook.* Richmond, Virginia: Virginia Department of Criminal Justice Services.

Benedek, E., & Cornell, D. (Eds.) (1989). *Juvenile homicide.* Washington, DC: American Psychiatric Press.

Borum, R. (1996). Improving the clinical practice of violence risk assessment: Technologies, guidelines, and training. *American Psychologist, 51,* 945–956.

Boulton, M. J., & Underwood, K. (1992). Bully/ victim problems among middle-school children. *British Journal of Educational Psychology, 62,* 73–87.

Code of Virginia, § 22.1–280.1(D) (2000).

Cole, E. (2003). Violence prevention in schools: Knowledge, skills, and interventions. In E. Cole & J. Siegal (Eds.). *Effective consultation in school psychology* (2nd ed.) (pp. 462–476). Ashland, OH: Hogrefe & Huber.

Cornell, D. (1990). Prior adjustment of violent juvenile offenders. *Law and Human Behavior, 14,* 569–578.

Cornell, D. (1999). Child and adolescent homicide. In V. B. Van Hasselt & M. Hersen (Eds.). *Handbook of psychological approaches with violent criminal offenders: Contemporary strategies and issues* (pp. 131–152). New York: Kluwer Academic.

Cornell, D. (2001). *Guidelines for responding to student threats of violence.* Charlottesville: University of Virginia.

Cornell, D. (2003). Guidelines for responding to student threats of violence. *Journal of Educational Administration, 41,* 705–719.

Cornell, D. (2004). Student threat assessment. In E. Gerler (Ed.). *Handbook of school violence* (pp. 115–136). Binghamton, NY: Haworth.

Cornell, D. (2005). School violence: Fears versus facts. In K. Heilbrun, N. Goldstein, & R. Redding (Eds.). *Juvenile delinquency: Prevention, assessment, and intervention* (pp. 45–66). New York: Oxford University Press.

Cornell, D., Benedek, E., & Benedek, D. (1987). Juvenile homicide: Prior adjustment and a proposed typology. *American Journal of Orthopsychiatry, 57,* 383–393.

Cornell, D., Cole, J., & Sheras, P. (in press). Assessment of bullying. In S. Jimerson & M. Furlong (Eds.). *Handbook of school violence and school safety: From research to practice.* Hillsdale, NJ: Erlbaum.

Cornell, D., & Loper, A. B. (1998). Assessment of violence and other high-risk behaviors with a school survey. *School Psychology Review, 27,* 317–330.

Cornell, D., Sheras, P., Kaplan, S., Levy-Elkon, A., McConville, D., McKnight, L., & Posey, J. (2004). Guidelines for responding to student threats of violence: Field test of a threat assessment approach. In M. J. Furlong, P. M. Kingery, & M. P. Bates (Eds.). *Appraisal and prediction of school violence: Context, issues, and methods* (pp. 11–36). Hauppauge, NY: Nova Science.

Cornell, D., Sheras, P. Kaplan, S., McConville, D., Posey, J., Levy-Elkon, A., McKnight, L., Branson, C., & Cole, J. (2004). Guidelines for student threat assessment: Field-test findings. *School Psychology Review, 33,* 527–546.

Cornell, D., & Williams, F. (in press). Threat assessment as a strategy to reduce school violence. In S. Jimerson and M. Furlong (Eds.). *Handbook of school violence and school safety: From research to practice.* Hillsdale, NJ: Erlbaum.

Cowen, E. L., Hightower, A. D., Pedro-Carroll, J. L., Work, W. C., & Wyman, P. A. (with Haffey, W. G.) (1996). *School-based prevention for children at risk: The Primary Mental Health Project.* Washington, DC: American Psychological Association. Available: http://www.childrensinstitute.net.

Craig, W. M. (1998). The relationship among bullying, victimization, depression, anxiety, and aggression in elementary school children. *Personality and Individual Differences, 24,* 123–130.

Crick, N. R., & Bigbee, M. A. (1998). Relational and overt forms of peer victimization: A multi-informant approach. *Journal of Consulting and Clinical Psychology, 66,* 337–347.

Davis v. Monroe County Board of Education, 526 US 629, 119 S.Ct. 1661 (1999).

DeVoe, J. F., Peter, K., Kaufman, P., Miller, A., Noonan, M., Snyder, T. D., & Baum, K. (2004). *Indicators of school crime and safety: 2004* (NCES 2005-002/NCJ 205290). Washington, DC: U.S. Departments of Education and Justice.

Drasgow, E., & Yell, M. L. (2001). Functional behavioral assessments: Legal requirements and challenges. *School Psychology Review, 30,* 239–251.

Dwyer, K. (1997). Disciplining students with disabilities. *NASP Communiqué, 26.* Available: http://www.nasponline.org/publications/cq262discipline.html.

Dwyer, K., and Osher, D. (2000). *Safeguarding our children: An action guide.* Washington, DC: U.S. Departments of Education and Justice, American Institutes for Research.

Dwyer, K., Osher, D., & Warger, C. (1998). *Early warning, timely response: A guide to safe schools.* Washington, DC: U.S. Department of Education.

Espelage, D. L., & Swearer, S. M. (2004). Research on school bullying and victimization: What have we learned and where do we go from here? *School Psychology Review, 32,* 365–383.

Family Educational Rights and Privacy Act (FERPA), 20 U.S.C. § 1232g; 34 CFR Part 99 (1974).

Farrell, A. D., Meyer, A. L., Sullivan, T. N., & Kung, E. M. (2003). Evaluation of the Responding in Peaceful and Positive Ways (RIPP) seventh grade violence prevention curriculum. *Journal of Child & Family Studies, 12,* 101–120.

Farrell, A. D., Meyer, A. L., & White, K. S. (2001). Evaluation of Responding in Peaceful and Positive Ways (RIPP): A school-based prevention program for reducing violence among urban adolescents. *Journal of Clinical Child Psychology, 30,* 451–463.

Federal Bureau of Investigation (1984–2004). *Uniform crime reports: Crime in the United States.* Washington, DC: U.S. Printing Office.

Fein, R., & Vossekuil, F. (1998). *Protective intelligence and threat assessment investigations: A guide for state and local law enforcement officials.* Washington, DC: U.S. Secret Service.

Fein, R., & Vossekuil, F. (1999). Assassination in the United States: An operational study of recent assassins, attackers, and near-lethal approachers. *Journal of Forensic Sciences, 44,* 321–333.

Fein, R., Vossekuil, F., & Holden, G. A. (1995). *Threat assessment: An approach to prevent targeted violence* (NCJ 155000). Washington, DC: National Institute of Justice. Available: http://www.secretservice.gov/ntac/ntac_threat.pdf.

Fein, R., Vossekuil, B., Pollack, W., Borum, R., Modzeleski, W., & Reddy, M. (2002). *Threat assessment in schools: A guide to managing threatening situations and to creating safe school climates.* Washington, DC: U.S. Secret Service and Department of Education.

Flannery, B. K., Sprague, J., & Todd, A. (1996). Including students with behavioral challenges: Blending school-wide discipline and individual supports. In L. Power-deFur & F. P. Orelove (Eds.). *Inclusive schools: A comprehensive guide to successful implementation* (pp. 227–244). Gaithersburg, MD: Aspen Publishing.

Forth, A., Kosson, D., & Hare, R. D. (2003). *Hare Psychopathy Checklist: Youth Version (PCL: YV).* Toronto, ON: Multi-Health Systems.

Furlong, M., Babinski, L., Poland, S., Munoz, J., & Boles, S. (1996). Factors associated with school psychologists' perceptions of campus violence. *Psychology in the Schools, 33,* 28–37.

Furlong, M., Chung, A., Bates, M., & Morrison, R. L. (1995). Who are the victims of school violence? A comparison of student non-victims and multi-victims. *Education and Treatment of Children, 18,* 282–298.

Furlong, M., Morrison, G., & Pavelski, R. (2000). Trends in school psychology for the 21st century: Influences of school violence on professional change. *Psychology in the Schools, 37,* 81–90.

Furlong, M., Morrison, G., Skiba, R., & Cornell, D. (Eds.) (2004). *Issues in school violence research.* Binghamton, NY: Haworth Press.

Furlong, M., Paige, L. Z., & Osher, D. (2003). The Safe Schools/Healthy Students (SS/HS) Initiative: Lessons learned from implementing comprehensive youth development programs. *Psychology in the Schools, 40,* 447–456.

Garrity, C., Jens, K., Porter, W., Sager, N., & Short-Camilli, C. (1994). *Bully-proofing your school.* Longmont, CO: Sopris West.

Gilmartin, B. G. (1987). Peer group antecedents of severe love-shyness in males. *Journal of Personality, 55,* 467–489.

Goldstein, A. P., Glick, B., Reiner, S., Zimmerman, D., & Coultry, T. (1987). *Aggression replacement training: A comprehensive intervention for aggressive youth.* Champaign, IL: Research Press.

Gottfredson, D. C., & Gottfredson, G. D. (2001). Quality of school-based prevention programs: Results from a national survey. *Journal of Research in Crime and Delinquency, 39,* 3–35.

Griffin, R. S., & Gross, A. M. (2004). Childhood bullying: Current empirical findings and future directions for research. *Aggression and Violent Behavior, 9,* 379–400.

Grossman D., Neckerman, H., Koepsell, T., Liu, P., Asher, K., Beland, K., Frey, K., & Rivara, F. (1997). Effectiveness of a violence prevention curriculum among children in elementary school: A randomized control trial. *Journal of the American Medical Association, 277,* 1605–1611.

Gun-Free Schools Act of 1994, 20 U.S.C. § 8921 (1994).

Heilbrun, K. (1997). Prediction versus management models relevant to risk assessment: The importance of legal decision-making context. *Law & Human Behavior, 21,* 347–359.

Henggeler, S. W., Melton, G. B., Brondino, M. J., Scherer, D. G., & Hanley, J. H. (1997). Multisystemic therapy with violent and chronic juvenile offenders and their families: The role of treatment fidelity in successful dissemination. *Journal of Consulting and Clinical Psychology, 65*, 821–833.

Hoover, J., & Oliver, R. (1996). *The bullying prevention handbook: A guide for principals, teachers, and counselors.* Bloomington, IN: National Education Service.

Individuals with Disabilities Education Act (IDEA), 20 U.S.C. § 1400 *et seq.,* revised and amended by Pub. L. No. 105-17, 111 Stat. 37 (1997).

Jacob, S., & Hartshorne, T. (2003). *Ethics and law for school psychologists* (4th ed.). Hoboken, NJ: Wiley.

Johnson, D. B. (2002). *Primary Project program manual.* Rochester, NY: Children's Institute.

K. K. v. State of Florida, 717 So.2d 629 (Fla. 5th DCA, 1998).

Kam, C. M., Greenberg, M. T., & Kusché, C. A. (2004). Sustained effects of the PATHS curriculum on the social and psychological adjustment of children in special education. *Journal of Emotional & Behavioral Disorders, 12*, 66–78.

Kaplan, S. G. (2005). *Threats of violence by students in special education.* Unpublished doctoral dissertation, University of Virginia.

Kochenderfer, B. J., & Ladd, G. W. (1996). Peer victimization: Cause or consequence of school maladjustment? *Child Development, 67*, 1305–1317.

Kusché, C. A. (2002). Psychoanalysis as prevention: Using PATHS to enhance ego development, object relationships, and cortical integration in children. *Journal of Applied Psychoanalytic Studies, 4*, 283–301.

Kusché, C. A., & Greenberg, M. T. (1994). *PATHS: Promoting Alternative THinking Strategies.* South Deerfield, MA: Channing Bete. Available: http://www.channing-bete.com/positiveyouth/pages/PATHS/PATHS.html.

Lantieri, L. (2003). Waging peace in our schools: The Resolving Conflict Creatively Program. In M. J. Elias, H. Arnold, & C. S. Hussey (Eds.). *EQ + IQ = best leadership practices for caring and successful schools* (pp. 76–88). Thousand Oaks, CA: Corwin Press.

Lantieri, L., DeJong, W., & Dutrey, J. (1996). Waging peace in our schools: The Resolving Conflict Creatively Program. In A. M. Hoffman (Ed.). *Schools, violence, and society* (pp. 241–251). Westport, CT: Praeger Publishers/Greenwood Publishing Group.

Larson, J., Smith, D., & Furlong, M. (2001). School violence. In A. Thomas (Ed.). *Best practices in school psychology III.* Washington, DC: National Association of School Psychologists.

Limber, S. P., & Small, M. A. (2003). State laws and policies to address bullying in schools. *School Psychology Review, 32*, 445–455.

Mayer, G. R. (1995). Preventing antisocial behavior in the schools. *Journal of Applied Behavior Analysis, 28*, 467–478.

Metzler, C. W., Biglan, A., Rusby, J. C., & Sprague, J. (2001). Evaluation of a comprehensive behavior management program to improve school-wide positive behavior support. *Education & Treatment of Children, 24*, 448–479.

Meyer, A., Farrell, A., Northup, W., Kung, E., & Plybon, L. (2000). *Promoting non-violence in early adolescence: Responding in peaceful and positive ways.* New York: Kluwer Academic/Plenum Press.

Miller, A. K. (2003). *Violence in U.S. public schools: 2000 school survey on crime and safety* (NCES 2004-314). Washington, DC: U.S. Department of Education, National Center for Education Statistics.

Milligan v. City of Slidell, 226 F.3d 652, 655 (5th Cir. 2000).

Mulvey, E. P., & Cauffman, E. (2001). The inherent limits of predicting school violence. *American Psychologist, 56,* 797–802.

Murrie, D., Cornell, D., Kaplan, S., McConville, S., & Levy-Elkon, A. (2004). Psychopathy scores and violence among juvenile offenders: A multi-measure study. *Behavioral Sciences & the Law, 22,* 49–67.

Nansel, T., Overpeck, M., Pilla, R., Ruan, W., Simons-Morton, B., & Scheidt, P. (2001). Bullying behaviors among US youth: Prevalence and association with psychosocial adjustment. *American Medical Association, 285,* 2094–2100.

National School Safety Center (1998). Checklist of characteristics of youth who have caused school-associated violent deaths. Westlake Village, CA: Author. Available: http://www.nssc1.org/reporter/checklist.htm.

National School Safety Center (2003). *School associated violent deaths.* Westlake Village, CA: Author. Available: http://www.nssc1.org/savd/savd.pdf.

Neary, A., & Joseph, S. (1994). Peer victimization and its relationship to self-concept and depression among schoolchildren. *Personality and Individual Differences, 16,* 183–196.

Nelson, J. R., Roberts, M. L., & Smith, D. J. (1998). *Conducting functional behavioral assessments: A practical guide.* Longmont, CO: Sopris West.

New Jersey v. T.L.O., 469 US 325 (1985).

No Child Left Behind Act of 2001, Pub. L., No. 107-110, § 1111–1112, 115 Stat. 1425 (2002).

Olweus, D. (1993). *Bullying at school: What we know and what we can do.* Oxford, UK: Blackwell.

Olweus, D., Limber, S., & Mihalic, S. F. (1999). *Blueprints for violence prevention—Book nine: Bullying prevention program.* Boulder, CO: Center for the Study and Prevention of Violence.

O'Neill, R. E., Horner, R. H., Albin, R. W., Sprague, J., Storey, K., & Newton, J. S. (1997). *Functional assessment and program development for problem behavior: A practical handbook* (2nd ed.). Pacific Grove, CA: Brooks/Cole.

Oppitz, J. L. (2003). Violence prevention: Empowering school counselors—A study of strategies used by practicing elementary school teachers. *Dissertation Abstracts International, 63*(8-A).

Ornelas v. United States, 517 U.S. 690, 697 (1996).

Osher, D., Dwyer, K., & Jackson, S. (2004). *Safe, supportive, and successful schools step by step.* Longmont, CO: Sopris West.

O'Toole, M. E. (2000). *The school shooter: A threat assessment perspective.* Quantico, VA: National Center for the Analysis of Violent Crime, Federal Bureau of Investigation.

Reddy, M., Borum, R., Berglund, J., Vossekuil, B., Fein, R., & Modzeleski, W. (2001). Evaluating risk for targeted violence in school: Comparing risk assessment, threat assessment, and other approaches. *Psychology in the Schools, 38,* 157–172.

Sewell, K. W., & Mendelsohn, M. (2000). Profiling potentially violent youth: Statistical and conceptual problems. *Children's Services: Social Policy, Research, and Practice, 3,* 147–169.

Sheras, P. L. (2002). *Your child: Bully or victim? Understanding and ending school yard tyranny.* New York: Skyline Press.

Shure, M. B. (1992). *I can problem solve (ICPS): An interpersonal cognitive problem solving program.* Champaign, IL: Research Press. Available: http://www.researchpress.com.

Shure, M. B. (1996a). *Raising a thinking child: Help your young child to resolve everyday conflicts and get along with others.* New York: Pocket Books.

Shure, M. B. (1996b). *Raising a thinking child workbook.* New York: Henry Holt. Available: http://www.researchpress.com.

Shure, M. B. (1997). Interpersonal cognitive problem solving: Primary prevention of early high-risk behaviors in the preschool and primary years. In G. W. Albee & T. P. Gullota (Eds.). *Primary prevention works* (pp. 167–190). Thousand Oaks, CA: Sage.

Shure, M. B. (2001). I can problem solve (ICPS): An interpersonal cognitive problem solving program for children. In S. I. Pfeiffer & L. A. Reddy (Eds.). *Innovative mental health interventions for children: Programs that work* (pp. 3–14). Binghamton, NY: Haworth Press.

Silver, E., & Teasdale, B. (2005). Mental disorder and violence: An examination of stressful life events and impaired social support. *Social Problems, 52,* 62–78.

Singer, M. I., & Flannery, D. J. (2000). The relationship between children's threats of violence and violent behaviors. *Archives of Pediatric and Adolescent Medicine, 154,* 785–790.

Skiba, R., Michael, R., Nardo, A., & Peterson, R. (2000). *The color of discipline: Sources of racial and gender disproportionality in school punishment.* Bloomington, IN: Indiana Education Policy Center. Available: http://www.indiana.edu/ ~ safeschl/cod.pdf.

Skiba, R. (2002). Special education and school discipline: A precarious balance. *Behavioral Disorders, 27,* 81–97.

Skiba, R., & Peterson, R. (1999). The dark side of zero tolerance: Can punishment lead to safe schools? *Phi Delta Kappan, 80,* 372–382.

Skiba, R., Waldron, N., Bahamonde, C., & Michalek, M. (1998). A four-step model for functional behavior assessment. *NASP Communiqué, 26.* Available: http://www. nasponline.org/publications/cq267fbamod. html.

Slee, P. T., & Rigby, K. (1993). Australian school children's self appraisal of interpersonal relations: The bullying experience. *Child Psychiatry and Human Development, 23,* 273–282.

Smith, J. D., Schneider, B. H., Smith, P. K., & Ananiadou, K. (2004). The effectiveness of whole school antibullying programs: A synthesis of evaluation research. *School Psychology Review, 33*(4), 547–560.

Sprague, J. (2002). Getting effective school discipline practices to scale: B.E.S.T. practices staff development. *Communiqué,*

30. Available: http://www.nasponline.org/publications/cq306best.html.

Sprague, J., & Golly, A. (2004). *Best behavior: Building positive support in schools.* Longmont, CO: Sopris West.

Sprague, J., Sugai, G., & Walker, H. (1998). Antisocial behavior in the schools. In S. Watson & F. Gresham (Eds.). *Child behavior therapy: Ecological considerations in assessment, treatment, and evaluation* (pp. 451–474). New York: Plenum Press.

Sprague, J., & Walker, H. (2000). Early identification and intervention for youth with antisocial and violent behavior. *Exceptional Children, 66,* 367–379.

Sprague, J., Walker, H., Golly, A., White, K., Myers, D. R., & Shannon, T. (2001). Translating research into effective practice: The effects of a universal staff and student intervention on indicators of discipline and school safety. *Education & Treatment of Children, 24,* 495–511.

Stafford, E., & Cornell, D. (2003). Psychopathy scores predict adolescent inpatient aggression. *Assessment, 10,* 102–112.

State of Wisconsin v. Angelia D.B., 211 Wis.2d 140, 564 NW.2d 682 (1997).

Sugai, G., & Horner, R. (1994). Including students with severe behavior problems in general education settings: Assumptions, challenges, and solutions. In J. Marr, G. Sugai, & G. Tindal (Eds.). *The Oregon conference monograph* (Vol. 6, pp. 102–120). Eugene: University of Oregon.

Sugai, G., Horner, R. H., Dunlap, G., Hieneman, M., Lewis, T. J., Nelson, C. M., Scott, T., Liaupsin, C., Sailor, W., Turnbull, A. P., Turnbull, H. R., Wickham, D., Wilcox, B., & Ruef, M. (2000). Applying positive behavior support and functional behavioral assessment in schools. *Journal of Positive Behavior Interventions, 2,* 131–143.

Taub, J. (2002). Evaluation of the Second Step Violence Prevention Program at a rural elementary school. *National Association of School Psychologists, 31,* 186–200.

Tebo, M. G. (2000). Zero tolerance, zero sense. *American Bar Association Journal* (April).

Trump, K. S. (1998). *Practical school security.* Thousand Oaks, CA: Corwin Press.

Trump, K. S. (2000). *Classroom killers? Hallway hostages? How schools can prevent and manage school crises.* Thousand Oaks, CA: Corwin Press.

Unnever, J. D., & Cornell, D. (2003). The culture of bullying in middle school. *Journal of School Violence, 2,* 5–27.

Unnever, J. D., & Cornell, D. (2004). Middle school victims of bullying: Who reports being bullied? *Aggressive Behavior, 30,* 373–388.

U.S. Census Bureau. (2003). *Statistical abstracts of the United States.* Washington, DC: U.S. Printing Office.

U.S. Office of Safe and Drug-Free Schools (2003). *Report on the implantation of the Gun-Free Schools Act in the states and outlying areas for school year 2000–2001.* Washington, DC: U.S. Department of Education, Office of Safe and Drug-Free Schools.

U.S. Surgeon General (2001). *Youth violence: A report of the Surgeon General.* Rockville, MD: U.S. Department of Health and Human Services.

Vossekuil, B., Fein, R., Reddy, M., Borum, R., & Modzeleski, W. (2002). *The final report and findings of the Safe School Initiative: Implications for the prevention of school attacks in the United States.* Washington, DC: U.S. Secret Service and U.S. Department of Education.

Wilson, D. B., Gottfredson, D. C., & Najaka, S. S. (2001). School-based prevention of problem behaviors: A meta-analysis. *Journal of Quantitative Criminology, 17,* 247–272.

Wilson, S. J., Lipsey, M. W., & Derzon, J. H. (2003). The effects of school-based intervention programs on aggressive behavior: A meta-analysis. *Journal of Consulting and Clinical Psychology, 71,* 136–149.